MIRACLE

on Southwest Boulevard

EUGENE FIELD ELEMENTARY

The Remarkable True Story of One Woman's Perseverance and Faith to Change the World, One Child at A Time.

A STUDY IN COMMUNITY SCHOOLS.

How To Turn A Low Performing School Into A Place of Academic Excellence.

Cindi Hemm WITH Katie Hemm Kinder
EDITED BY Lisa K. Lawrence Ph.D.

WESTBOW
PRESS
A DIVISION OF THOMAS NELSON

WestBow Press books may be ordered through booksellers or by contacting:

WestBow Press
A Division of Thomas Nelson
1663 Liberty Drive
Bloomington, IN 47403
www.westbowpress.com
1-(866) 928-1240

ISBN: 978-1-4497-1452-9 (sc)
ISBN: 978-1-4497-1454-3 (hc)
ISBN: 978-1-4497-1453-6 (e)

Library of Congress Control Number: 2011925112

Printed in the United States of America

WestBow Press rev. date: 3/22/2011

PRAISE FOR CINDI HEMM

"As principal of Eugene Field Elementary in Tulsa, Cindi has inspired and empowered teachers, parents, and students to grow and thrive."

-Carol L. Caldwell, Ed.D., Assistant Superintendent, Retired, Tulsa Public Schools

"Cindi Hemm is a best-in-class leader. She took the concept of community school and embraced it with open arms with a vision to make sure each of her kids had what they needed to learn, all day, every day."

-Former Tulsa Mayor Kathy Taylor

"Eugene Field Elementary was on the brink of closing down, enrollment was at a low point, and teachers were horribly discouraged when Cindi was assigned to our school. Within the first two years, the entire climate of our school changed drastically, enrollment grew, and the staff was purged of those who didn't share the Vision for our school community. Cindi has the highest expectations for every single person on her staff. I've never seen any one person bring about such a positive change in any school. She is the most amazing leader and our biggest cheerleader."

-Professional Educator, Gloria Newman

"Cindi has brought our staff closer and made us feel like family. She is a wonderful motivational leader."

-Professional Educator, Allison Nance Potteiger

"Cindi does whatever it takes to get the job done. I am amazed by her every day. God gives her incredible positive energy that she uses to manage, lift up, problem solve, encourage and build hope! Hope that everyone can truly accomplish whatever they can dream of."

-Support Staff member at Eugene Field, Lynette Dittus

I dedicate this book to two people:

To my wonderful husband, Jeff, of 35 years - I have loved you for 38 years of my life. We met when we were only sixteen years old and have had a great love affair ever since. You have always been there for me. Thank you for always telling me that I can stay at school "just a little longer" to get the job done. You wrap me up in a hug each and every day and I am at long last "home." I love you.

And

To Katie Vale Hemm Kinder, my precious daughter of my heart and my body. Without you, this work of love and labor would not have been possible. It is one thing to talk about writing a book, but another thing entirely to actually write it. You are a remarkable young woman and with your determination - all is possible! Thank you for all your hard work and long hours. I love you bunches and bunches.

AUTHOR'S NOTE

My mom, Cindi Hemm, is a remarkable woman. She has been going all over the nation to speak about how she turned a low-performing school into a place of academic excellence. A dynamic woman and gifted public speaker, her audiences get so quiet you can hear a pin drop. After she finishes her stories about her amazing journey, people come in droves to ask, "Can we buy your book?" She would shrug and say, "I haven't written a book...yet." Disappointed, her admirers would say, "You should!" I pushed her for several years to write a book, until one day she looked at me and said, "You should help me write it." My answer was, "Okay, let's do it!"

One night in early June 2010 as we drove to an out-of-town wedding, just the two of us, I brought along a tape recorder and made my mom talk for three hours about her school, Eugene Field Elementary. As I transcribed the stories and made them come to life on the page, I began to realize just how hard my mother had been working. Often times in the last seven years I felt sad or angry even that she was so busy, selfishly wanting her all to myself. But soon this project started seeping its way into my heart. I felt compelled each and every day to write continuously on this book. Pulled by a force beyond me I began to realize, for the first time, the many lives my mom has truly changed for the better. By the time I finished writing I knew in my heart that she is exactly where she is supposed to be, Eugene Field Elementary, changing the hearts and minds of the community and loving every student who comes through the doors at her school.

With this book I hope to reach thousands, maybe even millions of people who might never have known the courage, guts, heart, and drive of a woman I'm proud to call my mother.

Enjoy and God Bless,

Katie Hemm Kinder

Some names and events have been changed
to protect the innocent and the guilty

PART ONE

The Call

"The only journey is the journey within"
-Rainer Maria Rilke

CHAPTER ONE

The Beginning

The clock read 5:30 p.m. It was time to go home and cook dinner for my family. I sat at my desk thinking of the things I needed to do the next day. I made a quick to-do list and I packed my things away. Life was good. I was the principal at a middle class elementary school in Tulsa. Our test scores were good, my teachers were excellent, parent involvement was terrific, and my students would be getting out for the summer in exactly two days. My youngest daughter was getting married in July, one of my five children, all of whom were successful and happy. Born and raised in Tulsa and a product of Tulsa Public Schools in the 1970's, I felt honored to be a part of the district myself, as a professional educator. My husband, whom I married at age nineteen, was just as adorable today as he was 27 years before. We have the kind of marriage people dream of; he is supportive, loving, and kind. The year before we had welcomed our 5th child, an eight year old boy named Josh, into our family.

We lived a typical suburban life. The kids played soccer and baseball, and we ate dinner as a family every night and attended church every Sunday.

Yes, as I pulled away from my school, I indeed thought to myself that life was good. I had been at my current school, Park Elementary, for seven years; attendance and enrollment was at an all-time high. As I drove away I thought about the assembly that would be taking place the very next day. My fifth graders would be performing for the entire school, and I had invited the media to attend. I had confirmation that at least two stations would send camera crews. That was when I got the phone call that changed my life forever.

"Hello, this is Cindi Hemm,"

"Hi Cindi, we need to talk,"

Uh-oh, I thought, why would the assistant superintendent be calling me?

"How can I help you?" I questioned.

"We are so pleased with the job you have done with your current school. You have been there a long time now, and we all believe you have done everything you can with your students and teachers. We are reassigning you to Eugene Field Elementary. As you well know, this school is in bad shape. This is our last-ditch effort to try and keep the doors open. If you cannot go in and make some changes, we will shut the doors and bus the children out to different schools. Cindi, we felt you were the best candidate for the job."

My head was spinning. "I will go where Tulsa Public Schools needs me."

"Thanks, Cindi, we knew we could count on you. We will give you more details later. Close out your school year and get your daughter married, and we will talk later in the summer."

What? They couldn't mean the same Eugene Field, a school where the current custodian had been held at gunpoint and robbed as she walked to her car. The same Eugene Field that is constantly being broken into and vandalized. Where theft runs rampant. The same Eugene Field where the test scores are extremely low, whose children, at best, are latchkey or at worst poverty-stricken and abused. Eugene Field was a school whose parents were often non-existent, teachers are scarce, set in the middle of an entire community that exudes poverty. It was one and the same.

Eugene Field Elementary, I said it over and over in my mind. How could I walk in and turn it all around? Eugene Field had a 97 percent poverty rate where almost 100 percent of students qualified for Tulsa's free lunch program. It was also a school with a 92 percent mobility rate. Where kids just flat out don't stick around, moving constantly from one school to the next. Tulsa Public Schools had asked me to make the changes that would allow the school to remain open? How could I do that? I was only one person.

I drove around that night thinking about my new assignment. I thought about the time and effort I put into my current school, and how much more time it would take to tackle a school like Eugene Field. I thought about my husband and kids and how we raised them to do the right thing and put forth 100 percent effort in everything they did. And then I thought about a little girl and a little boy living in poverty. All they wanted to do the next day was get up and go to school because that was the only place they felt safe, the source of the only hot meal they got the entire day, the only place that included adults in their world who cared about them. I thought about this little girl and this little boy, and they represented my new challenge, my new calling: my new school. I believed, at that moment, that Eugene Field needed me and they were going to get 100 percent of my efforts.

Around the dinner table that night I told my family about my new adventure called Eugene Field Elementary. I explained to them, with poise, that this school needed me and I was going to do everything in my power to turn it all around. My kids gave their opinions and heartfelt congratulations. My husband, Jeff, looked at me and smiled with concern in his eyes. He did not even have to say it out loud, it happens sometimes when you have been married almost thirty years, I could read his expression; he believed I could do it. I needed nothing more than his confidence in my abilities and I was ready. Little did I know what was in store for me in the coming year.

The next day I skipped a principals meeting and drove across town to Eugene Field Elementary School. All the confidence I thought I had evaporated as soon as I pulled up. A decrepit old building passing itself off as a school was the only thing that greeted me. I drove around the neighborhood, if you could call it that; surrounding the school were three large housing projects that would make up the attendance area for my student population. Dirty and unkempt, my heart sank when I saw the disrepair of the school and the neglect of the property. Littered with graffiti, there were no signs as to where to enter the building. Tears stung my eyes as I found a place to park. I did not want to be here. I put my head down on my steering wheel and began to cry and pray.

"Lord, is this really your will for me? Help to calm my fearful heart as I begin this new phase of my life."

I reluctantly got out of my car and all of a sudden three heads popped out of the back door. One woman said, "Hi, are you our new principal?"

With a smile plastered on my face I hesitantly said, "Yes, I think so. I'm Cindi Hemm. Nice to meet you."

The school secretary, a woman whose position was the parent facilitator and a custodian welcomed me into the building, and I was given my first ever tour at Eugene Field. As they walked me around, they explained that their last day of school had been the day before and the "rooms were a little dirty." What I saw was more than a little dirt. Classroom furniture was upended, trash littered the floors, crayons smashed against the walls, and grime and dirt covered the entire building. In my twenty-four years of education I had never seen a building left in such horrible shape. I dutifully walked into each classroom and asked many questions, but the only thought running through my mind was, "Lord, I can't do this! This school needs more than just me!"

I asked the school secretary how many students attended last year. She said only 170 children attended Eugene Field last year, the lowest attendance in many years.

"170!" I said, "Let's just bus them over to my current school, Park Elementary, and I could stay where I am!"

She replied with regret in her voice, "No one wants our type of kid."

I asked, "What do you mean?"

She said, "They are not like the kids at your current school. They are rough kids, hungry and neglected, just like our building, but we are so excited you are coming. Everyone thinks you are the one to make a difference." Part of me wanted to scream and run away and never look back, but part of me looked deep within myself, I knew I had to do what ever was in my power to help these students. Thinking to myself there are no disposable children. No matter their income, race, behavior problems, background, the students of Eugene Field Elementary deserve a chance to make it in school and in life, and I was going to do everything in my power to make something of this run down, God-forsaken place. I thought to myself, Okay, Cindi, fasten your seatbelt; Eugene Field is going to be quite a ride!

The next day I had a long meeting with the Assistant Superintendent. I asked her what my number one priority at Eugene Field should be. She explained that my first job was to increase the student population.

"What about the dilapidated building?" I asked, "Are we sure that place isn't condemned?"

She explained, "Tulsa Public Schools will not build a brand new facility for only 170 students. Your first order of business will be to get more students through those doors, and then we can maybe talk about a new building." I thought to myself, "How in the world am I going to increase enrollment?" But what came out of my mouth was, "I am up for the challenge. I will not let you down." She told me about Eugene Field's current test scores, which were terribly low, and how attendance was also at an all-time low. I left her office feeling like the weight of the world rested solely on my shoulders.

After my daughter's wedding in late July, I broke the news to my current staff that I would not be returning the next year. Many tears were shed as I explained I had been called to a school very much in need and would be giving my all to turn things around in the Eugene Field community. I wrote a letter to all the parents at my current school telling them of my departure. I was so sad to be leaving such a wonderful school like Park Elementary. At that time in my life I really did feel like I knew what I was doing, and that I was a strong and capable principal. Little did I know I knew nothing about how to run an inner-urban, high poverty school. What I did know was how to pray and that is what I continued to do.

Many heartfelt goodbyes and good wishes later, I turned my attention to my new staff. I needed to put together a building leadership team with members of my new staff, most of whom I had never laid eyes on. I knew only one teacher in the entire faculty, Gloria Newman. Gloria had been teaching at Eugene Field for a number of years and I found myself in prayer yet again. "Lord, please let Gloria Newman be a wonderful teacher, someone I can trust, and depend on." I called Gloria, and she was extremely positive and genuinely pleased that I had been assigned to Eugene Field. I knew from experience that great leaders must rely on the people around them to be able to be successful. People who try and lead alone usually don't do it for very long. A strong faculty was a necessity for turning this school around and I knew that in my heart of hearts.

I asked Gloria to tell me about my new staff and to recommend two more team leaders. She looked at me with confidence and recommended two wonderful ladies named Marie Lenard and Brenda Knipfer. They are three of the most fantastic women I have ever had the pleasure to know. I can say with full confidence seven years later that my prayers were answered that day. Gloria, Marie, and Brenda turned out to be everything I prayed for and more. They still hold places on my school leadership team and very special places in my heart.

On that day in late July, 2003, I met with Gloria and she told me how moral was at an all-time low. The teachers were down on themselves and felt like neither the district nor the leadership within the school had any faith in them anymore. I listened intently while she told me I was just what her school needed, a leader full of compassion, with a backbone of steel and a heart for children. I felt so flattered she put such confidence in me, but I certainly had my doubts. With Gloria's help we assembled a team of strong individuals to make up my first leadership team that is still in place today. And thus begins the most terrifying, exhausting, exhilarating few years of my entire life.

CHAPTER TWO

Toxic

Entering my first school year at Eugene Field Elementary in August of 2003, I found the culture to be completely toxic for children, for teachers, and for the whole school community. On my first day as principal I arrived at school at 6:30 a.m. I was so nervous. A little less than an hour later a very large African-American woman, wearing a large t-shirt and nothing else, came traipsing, barefoot into the office. Stomping right up to the front desk, she started hollering so loudly you could hear her booming voice all the way through the school.

"Some goddamn teacher just grabbed and smacked my kid and wouldn't let him eat breakfast!" She screamed.

The color drained from my face as I said, "I'm Cindi Hemm, the new principal here. Please step into my office and we can have a conversation about this incident." This is a practice I still employ today, allowing parents to come into my office and vent if they need to, in order to diffuse any situation that may arise. I asked this mother if she had personally seen a teacher "grab and smack" her child. In my mind I was thinking, "Dear Lord, please don't let me have a teacher on my staff that would actually do such a thing."

The mom yelled, "Well, no, but my son ran home and told me and I believe him!"

I said, as I often do, "Goodness, if my child said something like that to me I would be very upset too." This allows the parent to feel validated, without taking sides until I hear the 'adult version' of the story. I calmed her down and let her know I would be getting to the bottom of this situation. I told her if she ever needed to talk to me again that my door was always open. I found out later that I didn't have a teacher on my faculty that would 'smack' a child. Instead, this particular boy had a habit of telling his mother false stories about teachers to see if she loved him enough to continue to 'yell at authority figures,' on his behalf. Oh boy, I wasn't in Kansas anymore.

The previous year, in my former school, I had led a book study on Ruby Payne's _A Framework for Understanding Poverty,_ and I remembered a certain aspect of this study in which the author explained one should always separate the child from the parent. Families from generational poverty tend to scream and yell at authority figures to show and express love for their children. I had never had this happen until now, but I was ready. I always ask the parent to come into my office to talk. I say, "Let's have a conversation, adult-to-adult first, and then we will bring in your child and hear his version of the story." More often than not, the child has left something out. In talking with parents, I always remind them that we are all on the same side; both educators and parents want their children to behave appropriately in school and learn the social skills that will allow them to be successful now and also later in their adult lives.

As the weeks wore on in my new position, I found there was never a day that went by that we didn't have a fight. Over the loud speaker several times a day I heard, "Mrs. Hemm, there is a fight in the south hall." "Mrs. Hemm, there is a fight in the cafeteria." "Mrs. Hemm, there is a fight in the bathroom, in the art room, outside at recess, by the flagpole!" Exhausted, I ran from fight to fight to fight, trying to put out fires, trying to discipline effectively, trying to fix this school, and it just wasn't working. I could hear cursing all the time and not just from the students; some of the teachers were aggressive and mean as well. Profanities slipped from their mouths incredibly easily, yet rarely did I see teachers or students being kind to one another.

One particular day I witnessed one student cussing and spitting at his teacher. I couldn't believe my ears, then I couldn't believe my eyes when the teacher grabbed the child by his ear, yanked him down the hall, all the while I stood in shocked disbelief that this was indeed my new school assignment. I naively thought I could put into place the practices I had used at my previous, middle class, school and be successful, but I was so wrong on so many different levels. The strategies and procedures that had worked in my last assignment were ineffective at Eugene Field. I realized I had to start from scratch, but how? I started with the quickest resource immediately at hand doing daily internet searches on how to discipline effectively in inner-urban, high poverty schools.

One day, early in that first year, one of the Eugene Field special education teachers came to me with horror in her eyes.

"Mrs. Hemm, come quick and bring the nurse!" She said frantically. "We have a little boy who has been injured."

With our nurse in tow, I ran down to her classroom. A multi-handicapped boy only seven years old, named Omar, had a gaping wound on his leg. "Oh no," I gasped. "Sweetie, can you tell me what happened to your leg?"

"Yes," he said softly. "My mama hit me this morning. She was mad at me. She has been takin' to hittin' me with the extension cord."

I became immediately furious as the staff around me collectively gasped. I looked at Omar's open flesh wound, caused by being beaten by an extension cord, and I hit the roof!

"This is unacceptable!" I lamented.

As our nurse and his teacher tended to his wound, I went into over-drive. I called the police. I called the Department of Human Services, and I made sure Omar would not see the inside of his so-called "home" ever again. His mother would never get the chance to harm him that way again!

As the day wore on I made all the necessary phone calls and filled out all the necessary paperwork to keep Omar safe. Police and DHS had found Omar's mother and let her know that Omar would not be returning home and that she was under investigation. Omar's mother did not take the news well. She stormed into the building and found Omar's teacher and starting screaming at her. Another staff member alerted me of what was happening, and I raced down to step in between the teacher and Omar's mother.

"Wait just a minute," I said sternly. "If you need to yell at anyone, it needs to be me. I am the one who made sure Omar would not be returning home today. Abuse like I saw today will never be tolerated at Eugene Field!"

She continued her raving and spewing venom, "You bitch! You don't know nothin' 'bout my son! So don't try and act like you do!"

"You need to leave the building immediately or I will call the police!" I said with as much authority as I could muster. Omar's mother took the super-sized Sonic drink she was holding and threw it all over my face and clothes, then turned on her heels and ran from the building. Dripping wet and sticky, I turned around to Omar's teacher and said, "Well, I bet you are glad I stepped in the middle of that or you would be the one wearing Dr. Pepper for the rest of the day!"

I held it together while I walked directly into the restroom to wash my face and hands. I looked at myself in the mirror, hair sticky with pop, outfit ruined, eyes haunted with the remembrance of the abuse I had seen on Omar's body earlier in the day. All I wanted to do was crawl in my comfy bed at home and never get out. The rest of the day the staff walked on egg shells around me asking nervously if I was okay. I shook my head and said, "It takes a little more than a crazy woman, armed with a cup full of Dr. Pepper, to keep me down," yet I knew in my heart that I was lying, simply waiting until I was in the safety of my own car to release the waterfall of tears threatening the back of my eyes.

Sure enough, as soon as I closed the door to my car, exited on the expressway home, my tears became wracking sobs of horror and exhaustion. I fumbled with my cell phone and called the only person I wanted to see in the world; my husband, Jeff. His voice had a calming effect on my hysteria, and by the time I reached our driveway and walked into our house, he had poured me a large glass of much-needed red wine.

"You can do this," he assured me. "They choose you for a reason. You have the perseverance, guts, and grit coupled with empathy, kindness and a willing heart to be able to do this job unlike anyone else!"

Jeff believed in me, but I continued to have my doubts about my own capabilities every day.

It came time for the school wide spelling bee. It was a ritual I was looking forward to because I had been a part of spelling bees for the past twenty-four years. I desperately needed something familiar in this new land I was floundering in. I prepared the night before and entered the gym the next morning with my previous expectations in my mind's eye. Instead, what I saw was horrifying. Appalled I watched the students of my school throwing paper wads, laughing and cutting up, some trying to fight. The contestants sat on the school stage and were also laughing, flipping each other off, and shoving one another. The whole thing was a complete joke. I made my way to the front of the assembly and took the microphone.

"Good morning, boys and girls. Welcome to our school spelling bee. I need everyone to get very quiet," I said naively, "This is a very important day and we will respect our spellers."

All at once the children started laughing…at me! Tears threatening, I did my best to pull myself together as I turned the program over to the teachers in charge of the spelling bee and I looked around. Not a single parent sat in the audience to watch his or her child. I couldn't believe it. This was not the familiar spelling bee I was used to. I had a sinking feeling when the participants didn't even care to try and spell words correctly. Jeering and finger pointing from the audience made the participants cut up even more. I grabbed the microphone.

"Excuse me! Teachers, if you cannot control your students, then we will dismiss the audience and do this without the rest of the student body!"

I thought this threat might calm everyone down, but it didn't. The children laughed at me and one child in particular yelled, "Hey, Principal, look at this," as he flipped me the bird! The entire student body simultaneously erupted in laughter. Powerless to stop the mayhem, I abruptly grabbed the microphone and with as much confidence as I could, I said,

"I will not allow this type of behavior at Eugene Field. Now, teachers, take your students back to class. We will continue the spelling bee without an audience."

The teachers were as surprised as the students that I actually followed through on my threat. We cleared the gym and were finally able to finish the bee and get our winner.

After the worst spelling bee in which I had ever participated was finally over, I went back to my office, shut the door, and sat glumly at my desk. With my head in my hands, and the weight of the world on my shoulders, someone came over my intercom and said, "Ms. Hemm, you are needed in the south hall there are two fights happening simultaneously!" I choked back tears and said, "I am on my way." I pulled my shoulders back and trudged onward prepared to put out yet another fire.

Three weeks into my new assignment as principal at Eugene Field Elementary, I was frantically called down to a fifth grade classroom. I ran down the hall and into the classroom to find our largest fifth grade boy, Marcus Lewis, 160 pounds of pure muscle and adrenaline, holding a chair above his head yelling at his teacher.

"That woman is a bitch and I won't sit here in her classroom no more!"

I was appalled and shocked as I screamed, "Marcus, put that chair down right now!"

Much to my surprise, he did what I asked. I told him to get to my office immediately. We walked out while the rest of his class laughed and taunted, "oooooooo new principal, what are you gonna do?"

Walking down the hall with Marcus, he cussed me up one side of the hall and down the other. I marched him into my office and as my voice started rising I sternly said, "Sit down in that chair!" He jutted his chin out and said, "Make me." I flew around my desk and he did something that had never happened to me in twenty-four years of education. He took a full swing at my face, and I did the only natural thing I knew to do. I ducked, swept his legs out from under him, and sat directly on top of him. Then I asked him, "Marcus, do you want me to call the police or do you want me to call your mama?" He completely surprised me by saying, "Oh, Mrs. Hemm, please call the police!" So I did what seemed logical to me and I called his mama!

She came trudging into my office, 300 pounds stuffed into a mini skirt and high heels, showing more cleavage than I had ever seen in my life. She appeared mean as a snake and mad as hell. I thought to myself, "Well, this is it. I am going to die right here at Eugene Field Elementary only three weeks into my new job!" I stepped up to greet her but she sidestepped me and got a hold of her son Marcus, and she did to him what my mama would have done to me had I cursed at my teacher. Though he might have deserved those first few slaps, I quickly intervened.

"Mrs. Lewis, we don't hit children in Tulsa Public Schools and especially at our school Eugene Field." As Marcus, our largest fifth grade boy, broke down in a fit of tears and shame his mother said, "Mrs. Hemm, you will not have any more trouble from my boy! Isn't that right, Marcus?"

"Yes, Ma'am."

And I didn't.

Soon after my incident with Marcus I made him my "deputy." Marcus would stop by my office every day and ask if I needed help with anything. The word on the street was that "Mrs. Hemm may look nice, but she is one tough principal!" Especially if she could take on both Marcus and his mama! A few months later Marcus was making his daily stop in my office to make sure things were running smoothly. I told my new deputy that I needed him to tell a kindergartner who was perpetually using one of our outside trees as a toilet that he couldn't use the bathroom outside anymore. Marcus, with a look of sheer determination on his face, said, "Yes, Ma'am, you can count on me." Despite the fact that we were in the middle of our state achievement tests and the building was actually quiet. Marcus immediately ran down the hallway shouting at this little kindergartner, "Boy, Mrs. Hemm says you can't piss outside no more!" I had to run after him saying "shhhhhhhhhhhh." Marcus repeated himself in a whisper, "Boy, Mrs. Hemm said you can't piss outside no more!"

"Thank you Marcus, but you can't say 'piss' at school."

"Yes, ma'am."

I walked away with a smile on my face. I was making little breakthroughs throughout the student population. That day was a victory on my part and for the school as a whole.

CHAPTER THREE

How to change the culture

Half way through that first semester at Eugene Field, I felt ragged and worn. To be completely honest, I thought I was failing. At times it felt as though the school climate was improving, and then something negative would happen and I would feel like I was right back to square one. I observed a sense of harshness in the faculty and staff. They had explained to me that the previous principal was terrified of the community. She kept all the doors to the building locked all the time. For years the former principal required her teachers to walk the children down the hall at the end of the school day and shove them out the door to their parents, always locking the building as soon as the students' backpacks cleared the door. It didn't matter if it was raining, sleeting, or snowing; students were immediately forced out of the school so the previous principal could lock up and get the hell out of dodge. Indeed, the school was right smack dab in the middle of one of the roughest areas in Tulsa. Nevertheless, this lock-out procedure gave the perception that the school was not safe. It seemed obvious that her former leadership style was still seeping into my staff, and I made it my mission to change that. It was an unacceptable way of thinking and I sought to change this way of acting immediately, but it wasn't easy.

One day I watched a woman, who was a part of the office staff, snapping at an adorable little second graders.

"No, you cannot call your mama and quit asking me!" She curtly shooed the little girl away.

I was taken aback that someone would talk this way to a child. Though being harsh was the way everyone had survived in this rough part of town until I became their administrator. It was time to change. I had many meetings about how the first order of business at Eugene Field Elementary was to be kind to everyone! Kindness to the children, kindness to the parents, and kindness to each other would be our new way of living while at this school. Any other way of behaving would not be tolerated. I also explained how we would be opening up the doors to the school and welcoming the parents into our halls.

"No more perception that this place isn't safe, because this is a safe place to be, a good place to be. We are here to serve the children and their parents and every single one of you will start behaving that way or you can find somewhere else to teach!"

I started getting parents involved in my school. Building upon the success I had with Marcus and his mother, I started employing parent involvement with other students and their parents. A few days after my altercation with Marcus, I was walking down the hall when a giggling third grader ran past me, stopped a few feet in front of me, dropped his drawers and "mooned" me at 8:30 in the morning on a Tuesday. I could lie and tell you I was shocked, but I wasn't. I picked him and his naked bottom up and carried him down to the office and then, what I did was call his mother to come and get him. And she did. This little boy never mooned me or anyone else ever again. Our parents were invited to get involved at Eugene Field, and I gained their trust by being kind and by being visible. My open door policy, that I still maintain today, started working wonders. Parents would storm my building ready for a fight because their child convinced them that the teacher was being mean. What I did surprised both parents and teachers. I would say, "Follow me, and let us sit and watch your child's teacher in action." In stunned surprise I would lead the parents into the teacher's classroom to observe my teachers and their fantastic abilities. By the time the parents left the building, they were not angry anymore.

We still had days where parents thought they could get violent in my halls, and I just flat out didn't tolerate it. When a pair of older siblings of some of my students started flying gang colors in my building, I had to shut that down and kick them out. Word continued to spread in the commuity that you don't mess with Cindi Hemm and her school. More importantly, word got out that Principal Hemm was not only tough as nails, but she loved each and every one of her students and would bend over backwards to help each one.

Little by little the community began to trust me and our faculty.

Beginning on my first day at school, I made it a point to walk into each and every classroom every single day, sometimes twice a day. I wanted to be seen as the leader of this school and not just heard. I wanted the teachers to know that at any given moment I might walk into their classrooms to see them in action. After a week of observation I walked in and took a seat in the classroom of one of our kindergarten teachers, Allison Potteiger. After I watched her teach for a few minutes I left the classroom, but Ms. Potteiger came traipsing after me; she was a woman on a mission.

"Ms. Hemm, am I doing something wrong?" she asked. "No," I said, "Why?"

"Why are you in my classroom?" She questioned, "This is the fifth day in a row you have been in to observe me. What have I done wrong?" She was so confused, not used to seeing her principal unless it was a scheduled 'official teacher evaluation.'

"Ms. Potteiger," I explained, "You are doing a great job, but I will be in your room every day. I want a feel for how you are teaching and how the children are learning."

"Oh," she said, relief coloring her voice, "Then I will see you tomorrow."

"Yes, you will," I laughed, "Now get back to your classroom and keep up the hard work!"

We began making strides as a school, but I was still the newcomer and I felt some resistance and resentment directed at me on a daily basis. I had to buck up, grow really thick skin, very fast, and not let it bother me, but it was hard. Since I was considered an outsider by some of the staff, there were times, they went behind my back, and to put it bluntly, would tell on me. On several occasions I would be disciplining a child in my office, thinking I had everything under control, when the parents would storm right into my office in the middle of my meeting with their child. Confused, I would look at them and ask, "How in the world did you know your daughter was in trouble?"

Triumphantly they would point to one of my office staff members and say, "She called and told me!" To say I was fuming was an understatement. I was being undermined on a regular basis. After many meetings and stern conversations, I got most people on board with our newly established culture of kindness at Eugene Field Elementary, but there were a few employees who wouldn't change their ways. Needless to say they didn't work at Eugene Field for much longer. I was there to help children, not to make friends. It wasn't easy to muster the personal strength to tolerate hostility from staff members. However, I had a strong group of friends and family outside of school and I had to remember that I wasn't the principal at Eugene Field Elementary to make friends, but to make a difference in the lives of children.

I was doing everything I could to create a feeling of safety and calm in our school. I began gathering information on many successful practices being used in other inner-urban, high poverty schools around the nation. In addition to re-reading Ruby Payne's _A Framework for Understanding poverty_, cover to cover several times, I began to implement another educational initiative drawn from

Susan Kovalik's <u>*Brain Based Classroom*</u>. Kovalik describes a best practice using only the colors you see in nature in the classroom. Kovalik explains children are calmer and better behaved when their environment has only earthy greens, browns, sky blues, and whites; teachers are encouraged to decorate with nature vines and plants. Teachers were required to use softer lighting with indirect lighting from lamps as opposed to the mainstream fluorescent overhead lights known to aggravate Attention Deficit and Hyperactivity Disorder (ADHD). Instrumental music playing in the background, clean and clutter-free classrooms, and good smells help children to calm down and learn more efficiently. I adopted this practice whole heartedly. The teachers were required to get rid of their clutter, and some of them were not happy. I had several teachers mad as hornets about having to instill this practice in their classrooms. Coming into my office and trying to convince me otherwise was like running their heads into a brick wall. I would say, "This is not a suggestion, this is a requirement. If you would like to continue teaching here, you will make your classroom a brain-based classroom to better serve our students." Many left my office in a huff and immediately called the teacher's union to complain about the bossy new principal.

Teachers are pack rats, and some of the faculty had been teaching at Eugene Field for twenty plus years. Their closets were packed to the brim with old worksheets, broken pencils, equipment, and boxes and boxes of complete crap. If it wasn't pleasing to the eye and they hadn't touched it in a year, I made them take it home. After days and days of cleaning, mounds of trash, foot stomping and all out teacher tantrums, our entire building had adopted a brain-based classroom on the Tulsa Model initiative based on Kovalik's work. It immediately calmed down the entire school, and I started getting less and less discipline sent to my office. It was truly remarkable.

One day, soon after each and every one of our classrooms were turned inside out and made into brain-based classrooms, I got a phone call.

"Ms. Hemm," my secretary said, "Sylvia Long from the teacher's union is on line three for you."

"This is Cindi Hemm," I said, knowing exactly what Ms. Long was about to say to me.

"Hi Cindi," she said, "Okay, what is going on over at Eugene Field that you would like to clue me in on? You were the principal at Park Elementary for seven years. Seven years, and not a single call or formal complaint was made against you. Then I get four calls in one day from teachers wanting to file grievances against you. Enlighten me, please!"

I explained calmly, "Sylvia, this is not Park, this is Eugene Field, and I can guarantee you will continue to get calls and formal grievances on me because I am going to make these people work and work hard! They need to do things right and follow my lead or find somewhere else to be!"

"Okay, Cindi," she said tentatively, "Keep us in the loop. We are also hearing wonderful things about you as well, and I know you can't please them all."

"We are changing lives Sylvia," I said, "Turning this school around takes hard work and people willing to give it their all!"

It became evident to everyone that I wasn't going anywhere. I would not be bullied out. I had high expectations and fully expected each and every one of my faculty to not only meet those expectations, but to exceed them. The culture began to change with the help of my leadership team and the open minds of my teachers. Together we were changing lives and making a difference and we wouldn't stop until we had the very best school in the state. We had a long way to go, as I would soon find out, but Eugene Field started to improve and look forward to better days ahead.

CHAPTER FOUR

Walk the Walk

"Mrs. Hemm," my secretary said through my trusty walkie talkie at the end of the school day, "You have a phone call on line three."

"Will you take a message? I'm making rounds to classrooms right now," I said dismissively.

"But, Mrs. Hemm, it's Josh."

"I will be right there!"

Josh is my youngest son, whom my husband and I adopted when he was only eight years old. He was waiting on line three for me as I hustled back to my office where I could speak with him privately. We had experienced a difficult "birth" when he became part of the Hemm family at the age of eight years old, because Josh was an abused former student from Park Elementary, my first assignment as a principal.

I picked up the phone, "Hi honey, what is going on?"

"Hey mom," he said, "I was wondering if I could go bowling with my youth group tonight?"

"Of course you can. Do you need Dad to take you?"

"That would be awesome!" He exclaimed.

"Okay, awesome," I chuckled, "I will let him know, but make sure you finish your homework before you head out!"

"Thanks Mom," he said, "I love you!" And he hung up.

Just a tad teary I said, "I love you back, sweet boy!"

Awesome was not the word to describe what happened to my youngest son back in 2002. After talking with Josh, I was brought back to the day we found out about the unimaginable abuse that was happening in his former household.

Countless hours on the phone to the police and DHS resulted in Josh being removed from his terribly abusive home. As the administrator at Park Elementary, I oversaw every aspect of what happened next. Charges were brought against both his mother and his father for harming their own flesh and blood. There was no other family member to take him in. He went directly to a shelter. My heart was broken for him.

I began to visit that abused eight year old boy every day. We played cards, games, and talked about how he was doing. He was so angry. And I couldn't blame him. Three days before the Easter holiday weekend I announced to my husband, Jeff, that I would be bringing Josh, from the shelter, home to spend the holiday weekend with our family. Jeff shrugged and said, "Okay, just for the weekend."

I immediately went out and bought him Easter clothes, an Easter basket, and truck-loads of Easter goodies. Josh was excited to spend the weekend with his principal. How special he felt to be able to have a slumber party at Mrs. Hemm's house, where he would be the envy of all his elementary school pals.

We had a great time. My whole family was in town to celebrate with us. Everyone got to meet and interact with Josh. As Sunday drew to an end Josh came to us and begged us not to take him back to the awful shelter.

"Please don't leave me in that place!" He pleaded, "I hate it there! Can I just stay with you?"

Jeff and I convened back in our bedroom without the ever hovering ears of our children.

"I can't take him back there, I won't, I can't. The shelter people said he couldn't even keep these new clothes, couldn't keep his Easter basket, they said they would trash all of it! I can't take him back there, I won't!"

"Cindi, be reasonable. We have four children, we are old, and we can't take on an eight year old boy."

On the verge of hysterical tears I said, "Fine, then you and Kenny can pack him up and take him back to that godforsaken place because I won't do it!"

"Okay," he said always very even keel. "You cool off and we will take him back to the shelter."

My husband and 16 year old son, Kenny, loaded Josh up in the car and drove away. Josh sat in the back seat, hat on backwards, clutching his new Easter basket that seemed bigger than he was. A silent car ride across town, Jeff and Kenny took Josh inside as the people at the shelter did exactly as they said they would and trashed his entire Easter basket. Jeff and Kenny left a crying Josh at the shelter, walked back to the car, throat dry and feet like lead. Pulling the car out of the parking lot and half way down 21st street, Kenny looked at his father and said, "We can't leave him there!"

Relieved, Jeff turned to Kenny and said, "I am so happy you said that. You are absolutely right," Jeff exclaimed, "Let's go get him!"

I sat on our front porch with puffy red eyes as my husband's white Crown Victoria came cruising down our street. Out popped Jeff and Kenny and then to my utter surprise out popped Josh, hat on backwards, crumpled Easter basket in his right hand, and I knew he would be our fifth and last child.

There was a little twinkle in Jeff's eye he looked at me and said, "Let's do this! You know that everyone will think we are his grandparents!"

"Speak for yourself," I laughed.

It wasn't easy. Josh, at eight, couldn't read, write, or spell. He had spent his entire life in survival mode which is not conducive to learning. We had a long road to haul. We took classes, we filled out paperwork, we disciplined, we hugged him when he didn't want us to, and we loved him when he didn't know that is what he was craving the most.

We were up again at 6:45 a.m. for ball games on Saturdays. Parent-Teacher conferences, soccer practices, baseball pictures, school clothes shopping, boy slumber parties, swim lessons, we did it all again. And were proud to.

I am happy to say that nine years later Josh is a phenomenal teenager. He earns straight A's, with the occasional B, a popular left handed baseball pitcher at Broken Arrow High School. But, most importantly, he has a heart of gold and a strength of character that is unmatched by his peers. Through his service to Christ, and to others he is our son through and through and we could not be prouder of him. Our fifth child, our baby boy, our Josh, how far he has come. And of course Jeff was right, when we are out and about with our youngest boy we are, indeed, frequently confused for his grandparents.

I was pulled out of my revelry when my counselor came bursting into my office with one of my students in tow.

"Mrs. Hemm," she explained, "Tommy's mother didn't pick him up from school today. Can you help us?"

Looking at Tommy's bright brown eyes full of fear and abandonment reminded me of Josh. Josh's story demonstrates that with a little love and direction, all students can be as successful as my youngest son.

"Come here Tommy," I comforted him with a hug, "we will figure this out. We will find your mama!"

CHAPTER FIVE

Getting Rid of Dead Weight

As I continued to evaluate my new school, the way it used to run, the way I was currently running it, and the heights to which I wanted Eugene Field to eventually soar, I had to really buckle down and start evaluating each individual teacher. I have only one deal breaker when it comes to teaching in my school: You must love children. Period. I didn't want a single teacher on my staff who couldn't be kind to children. I can say with complete honesty that the majority of my staff loved all children. Kindness mixed with firm discipline was the way most of my teachers operated. Children of poverty can be hard to handle, but you must encompass compassion with the ability to handle the children with love. It is quite a combination, but ninety percent of my staff had it down to a science. However, there were a few teachers who refused to work within our newly established culture of kindness, and that, I would not tolerate.

Insert Ralph Pride, our music teacher, an African-American man in his mid 50's. He had been teaching at Eugene Field for many years. Men can be hard to come by in early childhood education. When I first met Mr. Pride I was elated that not only a man was teaching our music class, but an African-American man who seemed to be a strong male role model. At Eugene Field Elementary School where the majority race was African American, I was so glad to meet Mr. Pride for the first time. I could forsee Mr. Pride being a wonderful example of love and discipline for the children of my school. Many months later I was so sad to realize I had been very wrong.

Mr. Pride had been the main disciplinarian for the last ten years at Eugene Field Elementary. The previous principal was all too happy to let Mr. Pride handle everything when it came to discipline. He ran the entire school. That was something I tried to stop immediately. I wanted to handle the discipline because I was the principal. I was the leader of this school. However, some of the teachers would not stop using him for discipline for their students, even though I had told them otherwise. They were so used to sending their so called "trouble makers" to Mr. Pride's classroom it was like second nature, and Mr. Pride would do what he did best. He would humiliate, ridicule, and make up names for the children. He did his best to shame the students into behaving. He demonstrated a despicable way to treat children, in my opinion, and also an unsuccessful way to get children to behave.

A couple months into my new assignment at Eugene Field I was walking by the music classroom when I heard shouting and name calling. Horrorstruck, I listened carefully.

"You stupid little girl! You think you can act that way in Ms. Ludoff's class?"

Aghast and livid, I listened in disbelief and silence, not understanding what was happening at first.

"Stop crying, you buck-toothed girl and start behaving!" Mr. Pride screamed.

I had heard enough. I stormed in the classroom like a Mama Bear wanting only to protect her cub!

"What is going on here?" I demanded. Mr. Pride looked at me like he was some kind of champion. "Well, Precious Matthews here tried to get into a fight in Ms. Ludoff's classroom. I was just teaching her a lesson."

I looked at Precious, normally a vivacious fourth grader, as she stood in the middle of the classroom floor on a red dot, crying softly as Mr. Pride humiliated her in the middle of his classroom of fifth graders, all of whom were looking on with a mixture of humor and regret in their eyes. Mr. Pride looked at me like he wanted me to pin a gold star on his jacket and tell him, "Good job!"

I was horrified and I said, "Precious, come with me, sweetheart, we will fix this and have a little chat in my office." I turned on Mr. Pride with fire in my eyes and said, "You will come see me in my office after school today!" He looked at me first with confusion and then with a challenge in his eyes as he said, "Yes, ma'am."

I still had hope for Mr. Pride. I thought to myself that surely once we talked and he understood that all student discipline first goes through me, and that under no circumstance would he ever be allowed to humiliate another student like that ever again, that he would step up and be the kind of leader I could count on. I really wanted to believe he would change his ways, but after numerous times continuing to catch him treating students down-right mean I had to start writing him up formally. I found him being mean to students, parents, and other teachers. He was one of the biggest bullies I had ever witnessed in my adult life. He would spend hours ridiculing children, making them stand on red dots as he made fun of them in front of other students. It was cruel, but I couldn't seem to get a hold on some of the teachers who continued to use him as their disciplinarian. He made the environment at school downright toxic, a place in which the only person, it seemed, able to handle kids was Mr. Pride. It undermined me. It also undermined the other teachers, and in return he bullied his way through the building every single day.

One day a few of our first-year teachers came into my office looking very forlorn and nervous. They said, "Cindi, we need to talk with you in private." I told them to come in and shut the door. "What is going on?" I asked.

"This is kind of hard to say and really embarrassing, but as I've spoken with a few of the other teachers," she gestured to the other women sitting in my office, "I'm not the only one feeling upset about a certain situation."

"Okay," I said, "What situation?"

"It's Ralph Pride, Ms. Hemm, he has been harassing us."

"Harassing you?" I questioned, "Like how?" These ladies spent the next hour telling me about how Mr. Pride would come up to them and rub their backs, pop their bras, pat them on the bottoms, and say sexually suggestive things to them every day. They felt uncomfortable. "We don't want to make a formal complaint because we don't want him knowing we are complaining about him. To be perfectly honest, we are a little intimidated by him. Can you help us?"

It didn't surprise me in the least that he was sexually harassing some of the teachers. He had been getting away with things like that for the past ten years, and it was time it stopped.

"Yes, I can help." I exclaimed, "Lucky for you, I am not intimidated by that man and I will talk with him, leaving your names out, of course, and I will write him up for this. He is absolutely not allowed to behave so inappropriately."

Ralph Pride was poisoning my school, and I was so angry! People were afraid to speak out against him for fear of what he might do. He was sexually harassing half the faculty. He continued to show up late for school, and the week before I had caught him sleeping with a pillow and blanket on the school stage during lunch time. I heard from another teacher that he had started taking naps, and I made sure I caught him red-handed. When he saw me coming, he jumped up from his little siesta and ran out the back door. I took his pillow and blanket, still warm, and threw them in the garbage. I continued to confront him and to write him up again, again, and again. A bully like Mr. Pride had been hiding in a school like Eugene Field Elementary because no one complained about his discipline tactics. He went right on screaming and yelling at children, bullying parents, harassing teachers, and doing exactly what he had always done. Parents were trying to find food to put on the table, and children were trying to survive. A bully like Mr. Pride was the least of their worries, so he continued his toxic behavior until I stepped in.

Well into my second year at Eugene Field, I was aware that Mr. Pride struggled with alcoholism. Coupled with rumors I had heard and his increasingly erratic behavior, I knew something was going on. I was keeping a strict thumb on him to make sure he was following procedure and not napping in the middle of the lunch room.

On a cold day in January, Mr. Pride had been late to school again and I sought him out to explain to him again that he was not allowed to show up late for work. As I approached him I could tell he was acting a little odd and as I continued to get closer to him I immediately knew why. It hit me like a truck. He reeked from head to toe of alcohol. He was drunk and I knew it. I called in two teachers, one I trusted and one he trusted, asking them to take him to a clinic for a urinalysis. After four awkward hours waiting in the clinic for the test results, it showed Mr. Pride to be legally drunk. Even though I knew he had to go even before this happened, it was still a hard day. I began the process to fire him, but before I could I received a phone call from Ralph.

"Cindi, please accept my resignation as of today."

"Okay, Ralph. I sincerely hope you get the help you need."

As many of my staff, me included, blew a collective sigh of relief, I got a second phone call from Mr. Pride.

"Ms. Hemm, never mind, I don't want to resign. I want to stay and teach."

"Ralph, I'm sorry, but Tulsa Public Schools has already accepted your resignation."

I was sorry it had to end that way. I really was. When I first met Ralph Pride I had such high hopes for him as a strong player in the rise of Eugene Field, but he continued to behave inappropriately. I also found out months later that he was stealing from our annual fundraiser for the music classroom. Ralph made off with over $6,000 of Eugene Field's money that the children had raised for the annual music fundraiser. As soon as he left and took his toxic behavior with him, the building became a much more peaceful place.

At this time the tide did turn. I was taking care of the school and handling all student discipline. I became the true leader. It went rapidly through the staff that I was a strong principal and would not allow bad behavior. Although getting rid of Ralph Pride was not the end of my problems. He left his stamp on the school and had a tight group of buddies who were mad as hell that their guy had been let go.

His best friend in the building, Pam Ludoff, was none too happy that her buddy Ralph was gone and she couldn't hide in the protection of a bully any longer. I hoped that with Mr. Pride gone, that his little group would shape up including Pam Ludoff. Instead, like the second bully in command she was mean to kids all the time. Horrific teaching skills masked an almost hatred of all children. I would walk into her classroom, and she mirrored exactly what Mr. Pride did. She yelled, screamed, and embarrassed children by mocking them. As with Mr. Pride, I didn't want to give up on one of our teachers. I tried and failed to find a grade she would thrive in. I placed her in kindergarten, and she continued her barrage of screaming. After I placed her in both third and fifth grade on separate occasions, she was still mean as a snake to her students. I came to the depressing conclusion that she would not change her ways.

A couple months after firing Ralph Pride, a mad Pam Ludoff came into my office and plopped down in the chair in front of me and said, "Ms. Hemm, I just wanted to let you know that I called Marquita a bitch!"

I sat and stared in stunned disbelief trying to process what she had just said to me.

"What did you just say?" I exclaimed, "You called a second grader a bitch?"

"Yep," she said, "And I would do it again. She was acting exactly like one. Anyway, her mama is really mad so I thought I would let you know what I said to her!"

I couldn't believe my ears as Ms. Ludoff sat in front of me with pure smugness in her voice as she relayed the rest of the story. She knew very good and well that behavior like that was not to be tolerated at Eugene Field, and she did it anyway with absolutely no remorse.

After diffusing the situation that most certainly arose with Marquita's mother, I immediately began writing up Pam Ludoff. I went after her job because that kind of behavior, being cruel to children, would never be tolerated in any school in which I found myself in leadership.

Life was rough on Ms. Ludoff for the rest of the year. While the rest of my teachers were doing wonderfully, working within our newly established culture of kindness, Pam and her hatred of children continued. Her poor choices resulted in her transfer out the very next year.

I understand that I am not perfect, and there are some employee personalities that clash with ones like mine. However, I am willing to work with anyone who truly has a passion for teaching, a love for children, and who vows to keep them safe while in school. If an educator embodies all three of those qualities, then our personal differences can be hammered out with respect. When a teacher calls small children bitches and are hateful to our precious students, then you better ship out.

The next teacher I had to go after was an entirely different kind of situation. It proved to be one of the hardest things I have ever had to do at Eugene Field or ever, for that matter.

Ruth McCormick was sweet to her students. She was a creative older woman with a beautiful brain-based classroom. She loved her students, but every day one of her children got seriously hurt while in her care. Bleeding, bumps and bruises became the norm for Ms. McCormick's students. It was quite disheartening so I began to spend more time stopping in her room to check things out. Bless her, but she didn't use proper English, she couldn't teach properly, and she couldn't meet her instructional objectives.

Ms. McCormick's kids were doing worse than all the other children in the whole school on bench-mark testing. I worked with her. I had other teachers work with her. I tried and tried to help her get on track, but it wasn't working. It was so hard because she loved her kids, and she was nice to everyone. We all really liked her as a person, but as a teacher she couldn't keep her students safe, let alone teach them the basic objectives.

State testing was looming over us, and I had to get her out of that classroom and let another teacher take over. Her students weren't prepared, and we had to prepare them for what was coming. I was going to reassign her to the library.

The day came when I had to call Ruth in and tell her I was changing her assignment. I was sick to my stomach. All day long I felt like I could throw up at any second. This wasn't like Ralph or Pam, both of whom seemed to want to challenge my leadership on a daily basis. This was a sweet, kind older woman, who loved her classroom and her children, but I had to do what was best for kids and she was not getting the job done. I called her in at the end of the day on a Friday with my stomach in knots.

"Hi, Ruth," I said, "Have a seat. We need to chat."

"Okay, Ms. Hemm," she said, "Is this about Jacob getting hurt in my class a few days ago? I really am sorry bout that. That silly boy jumped right off that desk and almost broke his arm!"

"Well, Ruth, it is partly because of that, but mostly because your class is not prepared for the state testing that is fast approaching. We have worked hard to get you on track, but it didn't take. I am changing your assignment as of Monday."

She burst into tears and she screamed, "Nooooooooo!" She sobbed, "You can't do this to me! My students will miss me and I will miss them! They need me!"

"Now Ruth, I am sorry we have to do this, but it is what is best for your students. They need to be given the opportunity to do well on the state test, and you will still get to see them when they come to the library."

Ms. McCormick literally flopped her entire body on my desk and wailed for a whole hour. Staff and faculty members could hear her screaming and crying as they walked by. After she picked herself up off my desk still sobbing she said, "You are horrible and you have ruined my life!"

"You are entitled to feel that way, Ruth. This is one of the hardest things I have ever had to do because, as a person, we all love you."

She left that day and immediately transferred out of my school. Relaying that story still makes me feel a little nauseated. However, with a new teacher in her class, her students began to thrive, stopped getting hurt, and started understanding their objectives for the state test. I will always do what is best for children. If you run into Ms. Ruth McCormick today she will still tell you that she hates me and that I ruined her life, but I don't hate her. I hate that I tried and failed to make her into a better teacher because she really did love her students. To this day if you ask some of her former students who their favorite teacher was, many of them will say, "Ms. McCormick."

I learned a lot from these three people. They have the dubious honor of being the only three teachers I have ever had to actually go after and job target to get them out of my school. As a principal, you can't have friends on your staff. You can love them. You can be kind to them. You can support them. You can go to their weddings and big events in their lives. You can pray with them, but you cannot be best friends. How can you go out drinking with your staff one night and then get mad the next day when they show up late and hung over? The answer is: you can't! A great leader leads. Teachers are the backbone of Eugene Field Elementary School. Teachers teach with their innovative ideas and creative minds. They are the most important person in some of our student's lives. Sometimes the only adult who truly show the students love are their teachers. Sometimes the only adult in their world who is consistent and constant in their lives and the only person they can count on is their teacher. Children growing up in generational poverty need strong role models. So I have to have the best staff in the state, in the nation, in the world.

And I do.

I would put our current staff up against any other staff in the world, and my money would be on them.

As long as I'm the principal at Eugene Field Elementary, I will always put children first and in doing that, I must have the best teachers on the planet. Academic achievement is the key to a positive future for the children of Eugene Field Elementary. I am committed to each and every child who walks the halls at this school. My priority lies with the kids.

PART TWO

The Foxhole

*"When things get tough, the tough drop to
their knees and beg for help"*
-Unknown

CHAPTER SIX

Test Scores in the Bottom of the Barrel

To an outsider it might have seemed like I had things somewhat under control at Eugene Field Elementary. I spoke with authority, I had gotten rid of some toxic people and behaviors, but I still felt like we were floundering. "Fake it until you make it," became my new motto. We were making strides, but, professionally, I was still very much in survival mode. Every procedure and instructional practice that I had installed into my new school still felt so very fragile, like at any moment it would all come crashing down on our heads if there was even the slightest upheaval.

Not only was I in survival mode, but so were my students. On a regular basis most of the children of Eugene Field were just trying to survive until the next day. The children lived with life or death questions of whether they were going to get to eat dinner that night, or if they were going to get hit by a parent, older sibling, or another adult in their community. School work was definitely not a priority in the least! However, once we endured the annual state achievement tests in April, I shoved my fears about our scores to the back of my mind because I had to close out the school for summer.

The day before the last day of school, an ornery ADHD little boy in first grade named Josiah was in trouble for the umpteenth time that week. His use of profane language was frequent and totally disruptive. I was physically and emotionally exhausted from the past few months, and I felt completely out of patience with Josiah and his continued poor behavior. I said, "Josiah, that is it! You are suspended for the rest of the school year! I'm taking you home!" I grabbed one of my teacher assistants to accompany us and put her and Josiah in my car to take him home.

I pulled up to a dilapidated old house where all the doors and windows were either wide open or broken. We could hear the television blaring from the car. Before I even stepped foot inside the house, the stench hit me like a ton of bricks. Animal fecal matter littered the front porch. I tried knocking, but no one could hear us over the noise of the television. I walked in. I couldn't believe the mess in front of me. I wanted to cringe and run away and never come back. My stomach churned as I looked around me. Dirty clothes were strung all over the floor. Mildew mixed with feces covered the walls and all over the house bugs were crawling on the floor. It took everything in me to not gag at the sight of this disgusting, filthy house. Then I saw a woman lying in some sort of reclining chair. She began to shout, scream and spit profanities at Josiah.

"Josiah, how dare you!" She screamed, "You filthy little bastard! You went and got yourself kicked out of school, didn't you!

More than outraged, I tried to interrupt. "Excuse me, ma'am?" But she didn't listen. She went right on with her tirade directed at her son.

"I can't even afford my medicine no more 'cause of your stupid medicine you haaaave to take! I wish you'd never been born!"

Little Josiah, standing directly in front of me, turned around, grabbed my skirt and whispered over and over again, "Ms. Hemm, don't leave me here, don't leave me here, don't leave me here."

It was one of the most awful things I had ever witnessed. I answered him immediately, "Josiah, no problem. We are going to take you back to school." I turned to the teacher assistant and asked her to put Josiah back in the car. "I'm going to have a word with Josiah's mother," I said. I waited for the car door to shut before I. Lost. My. Professional. Demeanor. I got directly in the woman's face!

"Now you listen to me, young lady!" I exclaimed with fire in my eyes. "You need to get up and start acting like a mother! How dare you treat your child that way!"

I continued my tirade directed at her. "When you have a baby, it isn't about you anymore!"

I continued. "Let me tell you something, honey. If I ever hear you talking that way to sweet Josiah again I will do more than just get in your face!" I looked over to her television for the first time and noticed she was watching of all things, pornography. I was livid, speechless, and my eyes began to well up with angry tears. The last thing I said to her was, "I'm not finished with you yet!" I walked out that door and got into the car and drove back to school. I held the hand of a crying Josiah all the way back through the doors. I knelt down and I hugged that first grade boy who was so abused, so neglected, so lost. "I'm so sorry honey, we are going to fix this."

I called the Department of Human Services, and they came and took Josiah away from that filthy house. Later that day both his mom and dad stormed into my office. They were furious that I was the one who initiated getting their son taken away. I told them the same thing I had told Josiah's mother earlier in the day, albeit in a calmer tone. I said they must clean up their act and their house to get their son back. And they did.

It was quite a day, but the day was not over yet. Sitting in my office, still reeling from the incident with Josiah, I got the news about Eugene Field's test scores, the news wasn't good. I knew we didn't do well, but I was shocked to find out how low our scores really were. We had some of the worst scores in the state. Later I would find out district administrators at the central office referred to us as part of the "bottom nine." I felt defeated and worn out. All the education literature and research I had poured over the last few months about changing a low performing school to a high performing school said I "had to change the culture first and foremost." How in the world was I supposed to bring up test scores when my students were hungry, abused, and neglected, just like Josiah? The challenge seemed impossible and I wanted to quit.

Out of a possible score of 1500 in Oklahoma, Eugene Field students scored a 288. We did not make adequate yearly progress. Here we were trying to change everything all at once at this school, and now we have to worry about test scores too! I could just hear my teachers complaining because I felt the same way. I was saying the same things in my head.

"We are doing the best we can!"

"We are trying to keep everyone safe!"

"We can't be expected to teach testing objectives when our children are trying just to survive!"

I agreed, but we had to try. We had to try harder. Something must be done. As the principal and instructional leader at Eugene Field, it was my job to lead our staff in the actions that would improve our scores. Yes, improving scores was the measure on which I focused because better scores would indicate that our children were learning. That, ultimately, was our goal: better educated children equipped with basic skills; the ability to learn, think, compute, and communicate, so that the students at Eugene Field would have the chance to break the cycle of poverty into which most of them were born.

I began my efforts by concentrating on pure data. I poured over the information day and night, trying to come up with a plan. After weeks of studying, it became clear to me that I had to meet with the teachers and together decide what to do.

I walked into the meeting and I could tell by their demeanors that my staff was tense. They were ready for the worst. I showed them our test scores and told them we had to do something to bring them up. They collectively shrugged their shoulders.

"Ms. Hemm, we are doing the best we can!" And they were. They didn't know how to do it any differently.

"Okay, guys, no more excuses," I said. "There are many reasons why our kids are not succeeding. I know you are teaching, but they are not learning!" I could see both defiance and hurt in their eyes. I would have felt the same way if I were in their places, but I couldn't let them see I was feeling the same way they were. I was their leader, and we were going to do better.

"We are working our asses off, and we love our students and this school, but I don't think we can work any harder than we are possibly working," someone said.

"I know you all are doing your best with these children. I know the hours you keep are long because I see when you come into work and I see when you go home. Most of you are working well beyond what is required by your contract. I'm not saying it will be easy, but we have to try and do it better," I explained. "I believe in each and every one of you, or you wouldn't be here."

I pulled out the data I had been working on and laid it on the table in front of the entire faculty. I showed them the information. If a child stayed three years at Eugene Field, he only moved up three months in reading. Unacceptable. After each one of our teachers looked over the data, they relaxed a little and began to understand the importance of doing things better. Eventually, hours later I had the entire staff sitting around the table with open minds and hearts, wanting to know how to change and what they could do better. Brain storming began.

We talked about how the building was much calmer because of the brain-based classrooms. What else could we do to help our students learn effectively? We started attending many professional development classes and programs. We decided we would employ a new technique, in which the teachers would teach to the level of the highest achieving student in the classroom instead of the lowest performing students. Teachers are kind, wonderful human beings or they wouldn't be in this profession. What many teachers do is stop everything if little Johnny doesn't understand the material and work solely with little Johnny, while the rest of the class twiddles their thumbs. Well, we learned that isn't an effective way to increase student learning. Instead of teaching to the lowest child in the class, a teacher should teach to the highest student level. As a result, the high kids get higher and the low kids get higher and so does everyone in the middle. In order to raise student achievement, high standards is what we were going to have. No more expecting to fail and expecting our kids to fail. We raised our expectations for everyone: kids, parents, and teachers.

Going into our second year at Eugene Field, I started to participate in every educational initiative I could get involved in, if I thought it would help us. We began an initiative called Compressed Curriculum. It is a best practice in which teachers present all the testing objectives before the students participate in state achievement testing in April, and then the last quarter teachers begin curriculum usually taught in the next grade. In other words, If a student is in second grade, the teacher begins teaching third grade objectives in the last quarter of the school year.

We began using "Raised Expectation Language." Our goal was to always be positive.

"You second graders are so smart and wonderful to be able to learn third grade material when you are only in the second grade! Oh my goodness, I'm so proud of my genius students!"

Our students would in turn feel so proud they would turn around and tell their parents how smart they were. In turn, everyone feels proud and continues to work harder and harder. These are raised expectations.

The parents of the students started bragging in the office about their children being so smart and learning above grade level. We could hear the pride in their voices as they beamed about their big brained children. This practice not only raised our test scores, but it helped our students gain respect in the eyes of the community.

Everyone in the building began promoting our school as the best school there ever was! We would say it all the time!

"Eugene Field is the best school in the universe!" The more we said it, the more everyone believed it to be true, and the more it became true on a daily basis. I would promote Eugene Field to anyone who would listen: students, parents, the media, members of the community...everyone! Students and families started wanting to return to Eugene Field. Enrollment began to climb and we started busting at the seams!

I wake up every day, as do the Eugene Field staff and ask, "How can I do it better today?" That attitude sets Eugene Field apart from the average school. We want to constantly learn how to better serve these children and their community.

That doesn't mean it's easy. It's never easy. Every day is tough. Every day at Eugene Field Elementary is hard because students such as ours, who find themselves in generational poverty, often lack basic human needs such as safety, food, and shelter. Their parents are adults who have suffered many hardships and for whom life is often a constant struggle. There are two types of days at Eugene Field, tough days and impossible days. We are lucky when it is only a tough day.

CHAPTER SEVEN

Don't Be Surprised When God Shows Up

One particularly horrendous day I felt ready to throw in the towel, call up Tulsa Public Schools, and tell them I was quitting. I was going to take up selling auto parts or some other routine, methodical sort of work because this job was simply too hard! Already that morning I had called DHS to come take a little girl out of a terribly abusive home. I had to suspend two fourth grade boys for bringing a pocket knife and brass knuckles to school. I had to call the police because a father of one student was threatening a father of another student out in front of the building. Stacks of paperwork needed my attention, and I had a line of students waiting for discipline from me. And this was just a typical day at Eugene Field. There was never a "light work day." Every single day, the duties of the job were extremely hard and demanding.

I arrived at school before anyone got there, and I stayed well after everyone left. I worked until 10 p.m. some nights. I was working Saturdays and Sundays. I was tired. Emotionally and physically exhausted, I put my head down on my desk one evening around 9:30 p.m. Alone in my office, I began to cry. I was missing my family. I missed going home at 5 p.m., and cooking dinner, and watching

"American Idol" on television. I missed my son and his baseball games. My husband and I were like passing ships in the night. I hardly ever got to see my children and grandchildren. I needed to pack up and go home, but I still had so much work to be done before the next school day.

Flailing and drowning in this new position of mine I literally got down on my knees on the office floor and prayed, "God, I need you and I need your help. I don't want to be here anymore. You must have a plan. This is the worst place I've ever been!" Still sobbing, bargaining, and wagering with the Lord I said, "Help me. Send me the people of God! Tell me what you want from me. What do I do? Why am I here?"

I prayed a long time that night, until I finally packed up and drove the 30 minutes home. Haggard and worn, I dragged myself inside and climbed into bed and finally fell asleep.

About a month later, my tearful prayer and sobbing that night in my office forgotten, a couple of members from the First United Methodist Church in downtown Tulsa came walking into my office. It is a church so big that the number of active members reaches up into the thousands. This church had been involved with Eugene Field since 1995. On what would prove to be a momentous day, these church members sat down in front of me and let me know they wanted to increase their involvement with our school. In the back of my mind, I remembered my pleading with God that late Wednesday night, asking Him to please send His people. And. He.Did.

"What do you need, Ms. Hemm?"

I told them we needed clothes, food, money, love and prayers for our community. They replied that they would give us anything we needed without hesitation and with a heart full of love. These generous Christian people offered to provide clothing and food without any bureaucracy, complications or conditions. It was fabulous. It was God.

A First United Methodist Sunday school class approached me and asked me what I thought the community needed. I suggested that they start having free community dinners at the end of each month, when the need was the greatest and food stamps had run out. Their answer was unequivocally "Yes!"

So on the last Friday of every month, members of First United Methodist Church drive up to Eugene Field in their Lexus's and SUV's, park in our parking lot, and serve the people of our school community with a heart for God. They feed them, serve them, love them, pray with them. This happens every month. Six years later, on the last Friday of the month, our gym is packed with people ready to eat, ready to be served, ready to be engulfed by the Holy Spirit. The Eugene Field community looks forward to the community dinners. Never once have I had to call security. Never once have I had to call the police during one of these dinners. It is a peaceful place to be the last Friday of every month at Eugene Field. Parents will walk through the halls to find me, "You having that dinner this Friday, Ms. Hemm?" I'm always so humbled to say, "Yes, we are. Come on down!"

But the Lord didn't stop with First United Methodist Church. He continued to send people of love into service at our school.

One day I was assembled with our school leadership team hashing out plans for the coming year. We were in great need of an early childhood education teacher. We had interviewed several candidates, but no one seemed to fit the "Eugene Field teacher mold." With only days left until the new year began, we were all feeling the angst of the vacant position. In the middle of the meeting, sitting around my conference table, with the leadership team, a beautiful young woman breezed through the office doors with a resume in hand.

"Hi, I'm Jennifer Samuelson." She said, "I just graduated from Oral Roberts University with a degree in early childhood education. I know this might sound strange, but I feel pulled to this school and I think God means for me to teach here."

We all looked at her and pulled our jaws up off the floor. We asked Jennifer to sit right down and interview for the position. She had a great interview, and we hired her on the spot. Six years later, she remains one of the strongest teachers I have ever seen in action.

She is a phenomenal teacher, leader, and person. We didn't know she was about to walk through our doors that day, but God knew she was coming. I firmly believe God sent her to our school. We needed Jennifer, and He hears our prayers.

These are just two examples of God's amazing work within this school. He continues to do wonderful things within the Eugene Field community. Why he choose me, a white, middle class woman who drinks wine and says the occasional curse word, I will never know. What I do know for sure is God is definitely working through me, and that means He continues to love all of us. Strengthened twenty fold, my personal faith has been tested these past few years. Ten years ago I would have described myself as a "laid back" Christian, but that has all changed. I know God has a plan for my life. I give Him the full glory for what has transpired at Eugene Field. I feel honored and humbled that He is continuing to work through me for this school and community.

I realize it may not be politically correct, but I am very openly a Christian. I do prayer requests at my faculty meetings where we share joys and concerns. I will openly pray for anyone who needs and requests me to do so. I adhere to the laws, and we don't teach religious doctrine at our school, but we do live it each and every day. There are no atheists in fox holes, and I was definitely in a fox hole.

As I drive up to school each day, I ask God for "Wisdom, Strength, and Knowledge." The Word of God teaches about faith, hope and love, but the greatest of these things is love. I often ask myself, "Can it be so simple as loving all these students?" I also say to myself, "Can it be as tough as loving all these students?" I believe so!

The past seven years as the principal at Eugene Field have shaped and molded the type of person I am today, and I wouldn't have it any other way. At least once every single day, and sometimes more, I ask Jesus to wrap his loving arms around Eugene Field Elementary. Protect us. We honor Him.

CHAPTER EIGHT

Target Teach and Benchmark Testing

Many schools in the Tulsa district had extremely low test scores. After our horrible test scores were reported at the end of my first year as principal at Eugene Field Elementary, Tulsa Public Schools got in touch with a company named Evans Newton Incorporated (ENI). ENI has a process called Target Teach that helps low-performing schools raise their test scores. We were strongly encouraged to use our school improvement money from the state of Oklahoma to hire ENI to align our textbooks and our teaching objectives to the Oklahoma state curriculum standards. I was shocked to learn there are sixty-four reading objectives in the third grade, but the state of Oklahoma only tests twenty-six of them. 26 out of 64. Mind boggling. I didn't know that, and neither did the teachers.

We developed a process we called "Power Objectives," and we placed the objectives for each grade in two categories. We had the "need to know" objectives, those that were tested, and the "nice to know objectives," those that were not tested. We taught the "need to know" objectives to mastery using at least four different lessons. We took the time to make sure each and every student mastered those "need to know" objectives. If we had time, we taught the "nice to know" objectives. Did we teach to the test? Absolutely! If the state of Oklahoma thought it was important enough to test it, we taught it!

Employees of ENI descended on our school in early January of 2005, and we started taking direction from them.

They took our textbooks and aligned them to the state testing standards. Most of our textbooks only aligned with the state test by 50 percent. In other words, only half of the lessons in the textbooks covered learning objectives on the Oklahoma achievement test. Our main math text, which we had just purchased, only aligned by 10 percent. Ten! We were sick about it. Soon, we discovered that most objectives were not even presented in our books. It was baffling to our entire staff that our teaching materials were not more closely connected to the skills our students were supposed to learn. When text book companies are creating textbooks that don't align with the state testing standards, something needs to change. Their content needs to be regulated.

I learned the hard way that textbook salesmen will lie to educators and claim that the textbook they are selling aligns 100 percent with the state standards. We often found their claims to be untrue. Some textbook companies do a better job aligning their texts than others, but 99 percent of all textbooks are written with California and Texas state tests in mind. California and Texas have the biggest student populations. Oklahoma students, as well as students in most other states, just get what is geared to those who live and test in California and Texas.

Working around the clock, employees of Target Teach developed benchmark tests. We were to make sure we were teaching the "need to know" objectives through several waves of benchmark testing throughout the year.

Target Teach staff also helped to develop lesson plans with the missing content objectives. They gave us extra lessons so we had ready-made successful lessons in hand when school started. They gave us packets for the on-level learner as well as packets for the lower-level learner. Their assistance, support, and materials were excellent.

Homework packets for the students were assembled in both English and Spanish for our Spanish speaking families. Target Teach and ENI were helping lay a foundation for eventual academic success.

We incorporated many educational initiatives to help the students at Eugene Field, but academically we used Target Teach. The practices that Target Teach embedded in our school became our academic backbone. After my first semester working with Target Teach, I am proud to say Eugene Field made adequate yearly progress for the first time in years. We began with a score of 288 out of 1500, and in one semester almost doubled our achievement scoring, 465 out of 1500. The heights to which we would eventually soar, I would soon find out.

Our teachers and students continued working hard with the lessons Target Teach had given us. We were teaching the objectives, and our students were learning. Benchmark testing was going smoothly, every couple of weeks, and we were on our way to earning better test scores.

One day in early March 2005 I was giving a tour of my school to a principal from a neighboring school district. As I was walking with her around the building, I was explaining to her the value of teaching the "need to know" objectives to mastery.

She stopped and looked at me and said, "You can't do that. That is cheating. You are teaching to the test!"

I started laughing and exclaimed, "Heck yes, we are teaching to the test. Why not? Let's set our students up for success!"

"Is it allowed?" asked the other principal.

"Absolutely," I said, "Here is the number and contact information for ENI's Target Teach."

Active learning was still occurring in our classrooms; we were simply adjusting our teaching concepts to include objectives from the state test. Yes, teachers should teach with mindfulness about the questions their students will be answering on state achievement tests. Questions are based on concepts that educators on state-wide committees have agreed are essential for the students to know and understand. The questions are not drawn from random or irrelevant facts and skills. To put it bluntly, "It's stupid not to teach to the test." And I didn't realize that until Target Teach came into our school. With Target Teach, our teachers weren't copying notes out of a book. We were using effective and interesting lessons and active learning was going on in every Eugene Field classroom.

In my opinion, every district could benefit by working with ENI to help align their textbooks and to also figure out what textbook best lines up with its state standards. I am and will continue to be a strong and enthusiastic advocate for ENI's Target Teach program. Academically, it works. If it can work at Eugene Field with our students, it can work anywhere.

CHAPTER NINE

Year-Round School and Uniforms

In the battle to improve the school climate and student achievement, struggling for almost two years at Eugene Field, I started grabbing hold of every initiative I could trying to make a positive difference in this school. A huge difference maker was when we went to Year Round School in 2005.

As I worked all summer in my office, as well as during winter and spring breaks, I noticed that the children in the Eugene Field community were literally running amuck. They would hang around the school. Sometimes the children were even trying to break into the building. The structure we had set up for them was gone and they yearned, sometimes subconsciously, sometimes not, to be back in school. School is a place in which they felt safe, where it is familiar, and where they are fed at least twice a day. We finally implemented a Year-Round School calendar. Why it took me two years to figure this out, I have no idea!

Children in extreme poverty aren't going to the beach during the summer. They don't take family vacations or go to church camp like my own children did during those precious summer months. Instead, they watch hours upon hours of television or end up getting into some sort of trouble.

Our faculty also noticed that our students were having a great deal of trouble retaining information learned the previous school year. For the Eugene Field students, Year Round School was the answer to that problem. Saying the words "Year Round School" can be extremely deceiving. We actually go to school the same number of days that students in other schools do. However, using a Year Round School calendar, the days are spread throughout the year so children can have a better chance at retaining information. We start our first day of school on August 1st. Our last day of school is usually in mid to late June. We have a three-week intersession in October. We observe a two-week winter break, a three-week spring break, and a six-week intersession in the summer.

During each of these "breaks," we have intersession camp. We pay Eugene Field staff through federal Title I money we receive. The children get to continue coming to the safest, best place they know: school.

To walk in to one of our intersessions is like taking a walk through childhood. Hiking trips, adventure walks, and arts and crafts are just a few of the activities set up for this special time. Laughter fills the hallways as the children learn how to cook their own food, play kickball, and roast marshmallows over the school fire pit. Walking down to the river learning about rocks, trees, and nature keep the children's minds set on continuous learning. Children are not sitting around dirty, unkempt apartments watching violence on television. Instead, the children are learning and being loved by the staff at Eugene Field Elementary.

A Year Round School calendar is highly recommend it to any school dealing with extreme poverty. It works. Staff members and faculty have to work a little harder, but it is worth it to see the joy on the faces of our students.

Another initiative I adopted whole heartedly was requiring the entire student population at Eugene Field to wear school uniforms.

Uniforms are the great equalizer. I noticed even in a community as poor as ours, we still had the "haves," and the "have not's." There were parents who took care of their children's clothes and there were the parents who, unfortunately, did not. Students as young as third, fourth and fifth grade were wearing gang colors and gang memorabilia. Typical school dress code wasn't working and I had to do something about it.

As I disciplined a little girl for making fun of another girl who wore a tank top in December, I thought to myself, "We need uniforms."

"The private middle schools and high schools wear uniforms. Why not our elementary school students?"

We had one problem: we didn't have the funds necessary to purchase uniforms and I couldn't expect parents to buy uniforms for their children when they didn't even have money for food. I went over to First United Methodist Church and asked for help. I barely got the words out of my mouth before they said, "Absolutely! We will help you!"

First United Methodist Church raised $12,000 dollars for school uniforms and then handed me a check. Every single child got three brand new uniforms for free. Every year the members of First United Methodist Church raise money to make sure each student gets uniforms at absolutely no cost to their families. And can I get an, "Amen!"

Only certain clothing colors are allowed and the students must wear their uniforms every day. It is required. Uniforms immediately calmed down our building. Discipline problems went down by ten percent, and I no longer had to worry about gang colors or the haves and the have not's.

Uniforms: The Great Equalizer. Also something I recommend for any school aimed for success.

CHAPTER TEN

Best Practice

I had noticed my first couple years at Eugene Field that we had to make the events of each school day consistent for the students or they would go absolutely bonkers. A small argument over who was next in the lunch line would break out into an all-out fist fight complete with blood and lost teeth. It was awful.

We looked at a national trend called PBS or Positive Behavior Support which taught us to use common language and procedures throughout the school. All adults were taught the procedures so that if faculty was in the office, cafeteria, or classroom, the procedures were all the same.

I started insisting everyone in the building start using common language for procedures. Therefore we have common procedures and language to go with it. Whether a student is in first grade or fifth they understand every procedure, the language that goes with that. Any adult in the building, if the student is in his class or not, knows who, what, where, and how to behave while in our school.

Everything we say is stated in positive terms. Instead of yelling, "Stop running!" We say, "Please walk."

There is a procedure for everything. As soon as a child walks through the doors, he puts his bag in his locker and immediately sits in the middle hallway with his class. At 7:30 a.m. the entire school goes into the gym, where we begin our day as a family. During our "Rise and Shine" Assembly, different school leaders take turns leading the school in announcements, performances and recognitions. The assembly lasts about 20 minutes. "Rise and Shine" is a practice we adopted from the "Great Expectation School Model," where the school day begins on a positive note and is something the children can count on each and every day. After the assembly, the children pick up their breakfasts and go into their classrooms with their teacher, to eat together as a family unit. This is where they begin their day of learning with, sometimes, the only consistent and loving adult in their lives: their teacher.

Consistency is key in the lives of children who exist within extreme poverty. Our students' lives are never consistent. Most of our kids live their lives around adults they can't trust. People who exist within generational poverty tend to make promises they can't keep, such as promises to buy birthday presents, move away, buy groceries. Never following through on their promises has lead the children of generational poverty to learn not to trust adults, unless they are at school. Eugene Field is a consistent, positive place to be and we do not deviate from the daily schedule. Children learn to just be kids, light hearted and happy; they know they can trust the schedule, always.

My second year at Eugene Field I was having a meeting with some Japanese educators in town for a conference. They couldn't believe here in the states that administrators would come over the loud speaker and interrupt the learning day.

"We don't understand why this happens in America," they said. "Breaking concentration and interrupting lessons to make an announcement is ridiculous."

And thus my "Rise and Shine" assembly idea was born. Every morning we start our day in a positive manner. This is the time we make all announcements and also the place where we celebrate our students' accomplishments, birthdays, and milestones. It completely eliminates the need for intercom announcements and interrupting classes and also starts the day off on the right foot.

Another "best practice" we put in place was having the Eugene Field support personnel adopt three different students each week. One third grader, one fourth grader, and one fifth grader would be chosen by a school employee who was not a professional educator such as a member of the support staff. They would check in on them, talk with them, and even provide them with incentives and treats. In turn, those students worked harder because they felt special and loved.

Common "best practice" procedures go on throughout the whole building every day. There are procedures for walking down the hall, with your hands behind your back, down the right side of the hall, and a bubble in your mouth (because you can't talk if you have a bubble in your mouth). The entire school walks down the hall this way and if someone steps out of line, everyone on the faculty takes the responsibility to correct the behavior in a consistent, positive manner.

There are procedures for the lunch room as well. When walking down the hall to the cafeteria, everyone must be in Line Order. I am telling you this now, every elementary school in the nation needs to be in Line Order. We instituted this practice in which each child knows exactly where they are to stand in the line each day because you stand in the same place, by the same people, every day. This takes away the, "She just cut in front of me," behavior because in a school like Eugene Field the, "She just cut in front of me," turns into an all-out brawl that ends up with someone in the hospital and I learned that the hard way. Line Order eliminates all that competition. At any time if there is a scuffle, all anyone has to say is, "Get in Line Order immediately," and our students scramble to their spots. The same people in front and behind you every day, all year long. Line Order is a simple practice that truly calmed down transition time. It is wonderful. It is consistent.

Another procedure we adopted was every week we put up a power standard for math and reading outside each classroom. The wording is in child-friendly terms so the children as well as their parents know exactly what the students will be learning that week. Everyone in the building knows what we are teaching every week.

These common "best practice" procedures help to make our school a family. Together we have created a complete community of learners without any one class operating by themselves without any feedback. We all work together as a whole to make our school function properly each and every day.

The development and consistent use of common best practice procedures is another element in the rise of Eugene Field Elementary.

CHAPTER ELEVEN

Positive Deviance

I am known as a positive deviant in my school and in my life. There are things I do because it is the right thing to do. I don't do anything illegal or immoral, but I don't always ask for permission, and I do bend the rules occasionally to help this community.

My whole theory is that life is a celebration. The more fun we have, the more we learn. Learning gets a bad rap sometimes. It doesn't have to be boring. It should be fun, and at my school, it is.

Any holiday we celebrate, we celebrate big.

In late April during my second year at Eugene Field, one of our Hispanic families came to me to ask a favor.

"Ms. Hemm, Cinco De Mayo is such a big deal in our culture. It has a rich tradition we would like to share with this school. We would like to have a celebration with authentic Mexican food prepared by several of our families for the entire school. Is that okay?"

Knowing I should go through the health department and get permission from the district, I shrugged my shoulders, nodded my head, and said, "Absolutely, what a great idea!" I exclaimed, "We can do better than that even, we will have a whole school day dedicated to

Cincode Mayo where we learn about your culture, have a parade, and at the end of the day have a celebration with decorations and food!"

Beaming, they left my office with a new sense of pride and humbleness that they were going to be able to share their culture with the community. Boy, did we do it up big time!

On May 5th we learned about Cinco de Mayo and its great importance for the Mexican communities. On May 5th, 1862, the 2,000 soldier Mexican army fought fiercely and won the Battle of Puebla against a more sophisticated French army of 6,000 soldiers. The observance of Cinco de Mayo is a special symbol for all Mexican people who celebrate their rights of freedom and liberty, honoring those who fought and won against great odds.

Our whole school was transformed into an authentic Cinco de Mayo celebration. The children had the time of their lives waving flags and noise makers in the parade. Our Hispanic students swelled with pride as they served the food of their people to their friends. We cheered and clapped and celebrated their culture, and everyone went home with a newfound respect for our Hispanic families. The food was fabulous, and the day was a wonderful learning experience for all the students at Eugene Field.

I wouldn't have been able to celebrate Cinco de Mayo with my school in this manner had I tried and failed to jump through all the professional hoops I was supposed to, but I'm not sorry because I did what would build our community and benefit our students.

Our annual Cinco de Mayo party is but one example of my positive deviance. Mardi Gras, Christmas, birthday celebrations, Thanksgiving, all have a part in making Eugene Field a well-rounded learning institution with the focus on children and what is best for them. You don't need a cape or an "S" painted on your chest. You don't need a special vigilante bat mobile to be a positive deviant, just listen closely to your heart and do what is right, which is not always easy, but I challenge everyone to reach out.

I do for my school and my students what I think is best for them because I'm proud to say I'm a positive deviant for Eugene Field Elementary.

CHAPTER TWELVE

A New Building To Call Home

By the end of the 2004 school year, we were busting at the seams with children. 300 students graced the halls of Eugene Field Elementary every day. It was a far cry from the mere 170 children who were enrolled at Eugene Field when I arrived back in the fall of 2003.

Our building was literally falling apart. It was in awful condition. The building was built in 1922 as a middle school. It was built the exact year a very affluent elementary school across town was also built, but that school was cared for and updated as needed because they have involved parents who took the time to make sure changes were made. Eugene Field wasn't cared for. Why would parents of Eugene Field care about an old school building when they were worried about staying warm in below-freezing temperatures with no heat in their apartments? They had life or death problems. A dilapidated old school building was not a concern to them.

In the spring of 2004, we had a very heavy rain season. One day when I happened to be working in the cafeteria, I heard terrified screaming and shouting coming from one of our first grade classrooms. Fearing the worst, I sprinted towards the screaming. Yanking the door open, I too started screaming because the entire ceiling had fallen in on the first graders. Sending prayers up, we scoured the room, pulling children out of the rubble and making sure they weren't hurt. Sifting through the upheaval, we came out with all twenty-three students, faces lined with dirt, grime, and tears. In some sort of miracle, nobody was seriously injured. By the sheer grace of God Himself, the caved-in ceiling had only hit the desks of the students, hurting no one, but leaving the building in complete disarray. The ceiling had been so heavy from the rain that the structure couldn't hold any longer. I was just so thankful the children were safe.

The next day I prepared myself for the barrage of angry phone calls and visits I knew I would be getting from parents, but I didn't receive a single phone call. I don't even think the kids told their parents what had happened, because stuff like this had been happening to them their entire lives. Figuratively and literally, ceilings have been falling in around these children at Eugene Field. I knew it was time for a new school building. If anyone deserved a new place to call home, it was our students.

Preparing my notes to meet with the assistant superintendent about plans for a new building, I received a frantic call from one of my kindergarten teachers, Brenda Knippfer.

"Oh my goodness," she yelled, "Cindi, We need you! Come quick!"

Panic inching its way up my spine I said, "Brenda, calm down, and tell me what is happening."

"The termites, the termites, they are swarming all over my room!"

"Really?" I said laughing, relief coloring my voice, "Cool, I'll be right down, I've never seen termites swarm before. Let's turn this into a lesson for the children!"

I shuffled down to Ms. Knippfer's room and the termites were indeed in full swarm. Ms. Knippfer looked at me like I had lost my mind and said, "Well, what are we going to do?" I said, "We are going to have a big school project on termites!"

Each class took turns watching the termites swarm. They were as intrigued as I was. As a school we spent the next few weeks doing an entire unit on termites. We had termite models in the hall, and we studied the life cycle of a termite. At the end of the unit we had a termite party complete with termite pudding (vanilla pudding with raisins). Every moment is teachable. When life handed us lemons, we made lemonade or in this case, termite pudding!

We called the exterminator and got the situation under control, but the termites had completely eaten away the foundation of our building.

In 1996 a 6.9 million dollar bond had been passed to build a new Eugene Field, but with only 170 students enrolled in the late 90's, Tulsa Public Schools wouldn't spend the money to build a new school if they were going to eventually have to turn around and shut the doors. By 2004, however, over 300 students were currently enrolled and it became clear the Eugene Field student population wasn't going anywhere; Tulsa Public Schools went ahead with plans to build a brand new state of the art school for our students.

We were hyped and excited to begin the plans for our new building. It was quite an undertaking. I had never even built a new house before, let alone a six million dollar building. As principal, I participated in the planning and went to countless meetings.

Flintco, a phenomenal company only about a mile away from us, was recruited to begin building the new and improved Eugene Field. Flintco, respected in the Tulsa community and all over the world, developed friendships with my staff and students. We took the construction workers food in the morning, donuts and bagels, and lunch in the afternoon. We had a parade over to their building and decorated their fences at Christmas time. Flintco, like many businesses and churches in the area spending time with my kids, fell instantly in love with the Eugene Field students. They developed an extra special interest in making the new building the very best! Building our new school was a really cool adventure for the whole community.

The day came when I was going to take the entire faculty in to see the new building for the first time being built. It wasn't dry walled yet, but the beams were up and we were going to be able to tell where each classroom would be. Our counselor Susan Burress, a very spiritual woman, who when I would rant and rave about something would look at me serenely, smile and say, "Let's pray about it." I would look at her hesitant and embarrassed and say, "Um, okay, I guess we can ask the Creator for help." Susan, bless her, would have me pray out loud. I was not comfortable praying out loud until Susan Burress came into my life. Now I'm extremely comfortable praying out loud and in front of large groups of people...Thanks, Susan.

Susan came to me the day before I was to take the whole faculty over to survey the new building and said, "Cindi, let's take Scripture over to the building, and write with permanent markers, Scripture all over the building before they dry wall and put carpet down."

"Susan, that is a fabulous idea," I said, "We will dedicate this new school to the Lord. As individual people, we will come and go, but if we dedicate this building to God it will always be His."

She went home that night and wrote out pages and pages of Scripture and brought them back with her the next morning. Armed with yellow hard hats, permanent markers, and page upon page of Scripture, we marched over to the new building. We walked in, gathered together and prayed, "Lord, we are dedicating this building to you. Always protect us while we are here, always protect the children. This is your building. Help us to keep evil out. Keep us safe each and every day, AMEN!"

We did the perfunctory tour, going from classroom to classroom, laughing and giggling about how great it was going to be to have a brand new building. Then Susan handed out the markers and Scripture. For the next hour we wrote, on every wall, every floor, every door facing. In the midst of our writing, I looked up to see the architects, bonds people, and all the Flintco builders gathered in a line around us. They were literally protecting and shielding us while we wrote words from Scripture on every pillar, window panel, flooring, and wall in the building. Several weeks later they dry walled and carpeted the entire school.

Think of it this way: God's words aren't hidden under the building materials; God's words are sealed into the very structure and foundation of the school, written there with the love and hope of the Eugene Field faithful. Every time you walk into Eugene Field Elementary, you can feel the peace of the Lord. I have had countless people tell me how peaceful and productive our building feels and these visitors think it is my doing, but I know it's Him. Even non-Christians who can't pin point or explain the peace and assurance they are feeling tell me how "Zen" it is to be at Eugene Field Elementary. One senses an atmosphere of peace as soon as you walk in. The school is a positive place to be, a safe place to be, and the best place some of my students will ever see and be a part of. I know Jesus Christ doesn't limit Himself to appearing in churches, because He is in my school, every day.

I received a phone call a few days after we wrote Scripture all over the frame of the new building. A gruff sounding woman said, "Excuse me, are you responsible for all this Scripture all over this building over here?"

Uh-oh, I thought to myself, I'm about to get in trouble. "Who am I talking to?" I asked.

"Well, I'm the night security guard, and I want to know who wrote these Scriptures!" She exclaimed!

I was thinking, "Why do you want to know? It's none of your business!"

I sat there on the phone in awkward silence until the woman continued talking. "Last night two vagrant, homeless men set up camp in that new building. They were drinking and causing a disturbance, so I asked them to leave. They wouldn't budge and started getting rowdy, on the verge of violence. I had to pull my gun out, and they finally got up and left the property. They didn't attack me or even come near me. With my hands trembling something awful, I looked up and all I saw around me was the word of God written all over the building. I had to call you and say thank you. Thank you for protecting me last night!"

"Ma'am," I replied, "I think you and I both know it wasn't me protecting you last night. It was Him."

We started the 2005 school year on August 1st in the old building, our first year to implement a Year Round School calendar, but by October our new school was move-in ready. The last day in our old building I invited the media to attend a ceremony in which all the students were going to give our old school a big hug. I also invited anyone who felt close to Eugene Field to be a part of the ceremony as well. We stood around the building, arms linked, and simultaneously gave the old structure a great big goodbye hug. It was adorable. We were closing down the school for our October/November intersession. We had exactly three weeks to box everything up and move it over to the new building.

That night, one of the last nights our 1922 school building was still standing, I called a special mandatory meeting for the entire faculty. At 7 p.m. 40 members of the Eugene Field staff walked into one of the old rooms, holding a candle. We stood around in a circle and one by one we lit our candles and told a story about the old building. We needed closure and to say goodbye. Even though the building was falling apart, it was still the place many of the teachers and faculty loved and called home to their classrooms and lives for many years. There were lots of tears shed. Some of the teachers, like Ms. Cephus, had been there for thirty years. We prayed the children would be safe during this three-week break from school as we moved. We thanked God for the many blessings He bestowed on us in this old building. For two hours we cried, prayed, and told stories. Then we blew out our candles and left in silence.

The day the old building was to come down, the demolishing crew arrived. A number of us stood around and watched as they tore down the Eugene Field of old. To our utter surprise, twenty to thirty huge rats came streaming out of the basement. Pandemonium ensued, everyone screaming and running in different directions. We immediately put rat traps around the new building to ensure its safety.

If any doubts remained that the old building needed to come down it was alleviated that day...Gross!

As the wrecking crew continued to demolish the building, I had the grand idea to bring in some of the structures from the old building into the new building to make it seem more like home to the teachers and students. I wanted the beautiful 1920's limestone scroll work. I called Tulsa Public Schools and asked, "Can I take some of the old scroll work with me into our new building?" I was shocked with they said, "No, we are going to put it in the landfill."

"The landfill!" I exclaimed, frustrated, "That is ridiculous!"

Thinking to myself how wasteful and unnecessary that sounded, I decided to take matters into my own hands. Sometimes I live my life by the motto, "Sometimes it is better to ask forgiveness than for permission!"

Throwing on a yellow hard hat and marching out to the wrecking crew, I started waving my hands all around. "Hello there," I yelled! The man driving the front loader stopped what he was doing to look at the crazy principal and said, "Ma'am, you simply cannot be out here! What are you doing?" he questioned briskly.

I crawled up on the front loader, adjusted my hard had, and said, "I need all this old scroll work. I need you to drop it off in front of the new building when you are done!"

He said, "No ma'am, that is not in our contract. Did you not hear me when I said you cannot be up here?"

"I heard you, but I choose to ignore you. Look, I will buy you and your entire crew hamburgers and malts from Sonic if you will drop all this scroll work at the new building before you leave today."

"You got it, ma'am!" He exclaimed.

For the price of seven hamburgers and seven malts, we enjoy the most beautiful architectural detailed arches and scroll work all around the new building. We are proud of the beauty and sense of history it evokes, a respect for and acknowledgement of rich tradition, and the enduring nature of our school building and its place in our community.

We continued our packing and unpacking. It was quite a move. We moved in record time, thanks to Debbie Schumacher, our own personal "Box Nazi!" Debbie delivered us a certain number of boxes, and she did not relent if we whined for more. We boxed everything up, moved, and opened the doors to our new state-of-the-art school on November 13th, 2005.

Our emphasis on students is visible immediately when one approaches the main entrance to the new Eugene Field Elementary school. Etched in the sidewalk are the names of all the students who were enrolled at our school in the fall of 2005. One of our big donors in Tulsa gave us $15,000 dollars to sandblast every child's name onto the sidewalk in front of our school. The tradition is a practice I copied from the University of Arkansas where my husband and I graduated from college. The University sandblasts each graduate's name on the sidewalk, where it remains today. Because my husband Jeff and I feel so proud to have our names etched in stone in the middle of Fayetteville, Arkansas, I thought my students would also feel so proud if we could sandblast their names on the sidewalk around our new school. The students are indeed very proud of their mark on the building and the fact that they, personally, own a piece of Eugene Field forever. It was $15,000 dollars well spent. The kids love it!

The very first day we opened up the new building, the students and their parents walked in and were amazed at how nice it was. One of my student's parents walked right up to me, wrapped her arms around me and said, "We have never had anything this nice before, thank you!" The children's first reaction to the new building was priceless. One said, "The walls are white, I bet this is what heaven looks like!"

This school building is not mine, it's theirs. The community takes great pride in their new school. Tears of joy streaming down their faces, the children jumped for joy and ran from classroom to classroom, high-fiving their friends and hugging their parents.

A few weeks later, up and running in the new and improved Eugene Field Elementary, an older gentleman came into our offices.

He said, so sadly, "Where is my school? I came all the way from Sallisaw to look at my old school and it's gone." I introduced myself to him and walked him around the new building, but it was not the nostalgic walk down memory lane that he had come to experience. The gentleman, a student at Eugene Field in the 1940's, made quite an impression on me. I decided to create a Wall of Memories for anyone in search of a piece of the old building to reminisce about. Covering an entire wall in our school hallway, our wall of fame includes many donated items such as old pictures, report cards, and stories from the 1920's through the 1990's. It keeps the memories alive.

The new building has been such a blessing. The children and their parents take care of the building. There has been no vandalizing or menacing behavior from the community because they are so proud of our new school and so was I. We were flourishing. What a whirlwind we had experienced from my first visit back in the summer of 2003, taking over a dilapidated building and meager 170 students. By the 2010 school year, we had over 420 students walking the hallways at the new Eugene Field Elementary.

PART THREE

A Community School

"In every community there is work to be done. In every nation, there are wounds to heal. In every heart there is the power to do it."
-Marianne Williamson

CHAPTER THIRTEEN

The Hub

Many years ago all the schools in our area of Tulsa, including Eugene Field, would close their doors at 3 p.m. after the dismissal of classes. Everyone would high tail it home. The school doors would only reopen again the next day for school. Windows and doors locked tight, lights turned off; no one was allowed to reenter the school.

I noticed even before we built our brand new building, our school was the hub of activity for the entire neighborhood. Often getting to school before 7 a.m. and staying until 10 p.m., I started leaving the building open for anyone who needed back in the school. I was there to serve the people of this community. Because the people took such pride in their school, it seemed that they should have access to it when they wanted. More often than not, I had members of the community coming to me with requests.

"Ms. Hemm, can we use the gym on Saturday to play basketball?"

"Ms. Hemm, we want to have a picnic by the playground on Sunday evening."

"Ms. Hemm, can we use the library on Friday night to read to our parents?"

Faculty and staff began to develop a whole new mindset when it came to serving these people. This was a public school with public dollars. It was the people's school, and if they wanted to use the facility on the weekend or after hours then they should be able to do so. If I personally couldn't be there to let them in, I made sure someone was at school so they could use what we had to offer. These people needed this school to be open, and we were there to serve them.

One Monday morning I arrived at work to a hysterical parent who had experienced a horrible tragedy over the weekend.

"Oh, Ms. Hemm, we need you," she cried, "Our house burnt to the ground last night and we have nothing! Please help us!"

And I did what any whole-hearted person would do. I said, "Of course we will help you," I embraced her as she sobbed, "Don't worry; we are here to help in times of trouble."

Walking through the rubble that had once been their two bedroom house, I saw the devastation first hand. We got on the phone and found clothing for her entire family, a place for them to live, and food to stock their pantry. We were able to gather resources that the family would not have been able to accomplish on their own had they not been able to count on us. They would have been left homeless and hungry without the support from Eugene Field Elementary.

I had noticed that none of the people in the neighborhood had any type of healthcare at all. These people were walking around sick, even with broken bones, because no one had money or transportation to get basic medical care.

I was able to recruit a doctor and nursing staff who comes to our school two days a week and sets up shop in our gym free of charge. Our Bedlam Clinic gives free health care to anyone who needs it. People come in droves to get checked out. In return, our community receives the medical attention they so desperately need.

I invited any agency who wanted to help into my school to serve the public. The Boy Scouts of America walked in one day and said, "Do you have any projects for us to do?"

My answer is always, "Absolutely!" So far, there have been thirteen Eagle Scout projects completed at our school, and many of the Boy Scouts' parents have become mentors at Eugene Field. Painting walls, building structures, and being mentors became the norm for many of the Boy Scouts wanting to serve.

It was also very apparent that the children of Eugene Field didn't get to participate in any kind of extracurricular activities…ever. Things like soccer, basketball, dance, and Girl Scouts were out of reach for the kids in this neighborhood. Activities that children from affluent and middle class families take for granted, we began providing at no cost to our children and their parents. We also sought out programs in which we believed our students would thrive. Eugene Field Elementary currently has twenty-six after school programs including, but not limited to, piano lessons, soccer, basketball, football, baton twirling, hip-hop dance classes, Boy Scouts, Girl scouts, and Campfire. We welcome any agency who wishes to serve us.

Our theme became, "How can we serve you?"

We simply did this out of being servants for others and not any greater purpose other than to just be kind.

When giving a tour after school one day to a group of educators from another state, I began explaining to them all the programs we were providing for our neighborhood.

They said, "Cindi, what a wonderful Community School you have here! So few schools are able to attain this kind of cohesive community culture!"

I tilted my head in question, smiled, and said, "Yeah, I guess we do have a Community School. Isn't that interesting!" It was the first time I had heard the term "Community School."

That night I researched Community Schools. The term is a current buzz word in education, describing a school in which faculties serve the community where their students live. Community Schools service not only the children, but their families. The Secretary of Education Arnie Duncan started the Community School movement, in Chicago and he did his best to serve his community. For years, good principals tried to do the same. Now Eugene Field has the official title of a Community School and we are known throughout the Tulsa area as a place that will help people. The Community School term is our umbrella as it encompasses everything we do and gives us a framework to work off of. There are now currently eighteen community schools in the Tulsa area.

I wish I could say back when I laid my head down on my desk crying out to the Lord for help that I knew what Eugene Field would become, but I didn't. I'm not visionary like God is. He is the one with the plan, and I merely led those of us who are carrying out His plan. God works through our school's superior staff and the many volunteers sent into service at this school. He is in charge, not me.

Good people serve others, always. Being labeled a Community School didn't make us work harder. We worked harder and loved deeper because we felt called to do so.

If you need some help, come on over to the hub. We will be glad to serve you!

CHAPTER FOURTEEN

Global Gardens

In late spring 2005, the daughter of a very prominent family involved in First United Methodist Church came to me with some grand ideas.

"Hi, I'm Heather Oakley," she said, "I've just returned home from living and teaching in New York."

When Heather mentioned 'teaching in Harlem' she got my attention and I welcomed her into my office. Heather, a very positive personality, infectious to be around, sat in my office for the next 45 minutes and told me about her background. She had just returned to the Tulsa area after several years teaching in Harlem at the United Nations School and wasn't currently working anywhere.

"My parents have been gushing about you and your fabulous school for quite some time," she explained. "I had to get over here and meet you. I want to tell you about my dream to build a community garden and teach children using curriculum based around science and nature."

Interested in her vision of a community garden, I urged her to tell me more.

"I want the children to have plots of their very own in this garden to grow food, plants, and flowers." I could feel the passion and excitement in her voice as she continued. "I also want this future garden to be made available to the people living in the low income housing projects to be able to grow their own food as well!"

It sounded like a great idea to me. By the time Heather left my office, we had put in place the plans to build a community garden right beside Eugene Field Elementary.

Knowing I was supposed to go through Tulsa Public Schools central administration and countless lawyers to get permission to do a project this large, I felt the task too daunting. Instead, I told Heather to go ahead with the plans to plow the land that sat right next to the school. This felt right and it was good for my school, good for the community, and most importantly good for the children. So I, personally, gave the green light. Months later our new community garden was plowed and ready for children to start literally getting their hands dirty.

Heather took great initiative as she taught the children how to plant seeds, trees, and flowers. The children were thrilled to be able to own a part of the community garden. Heather Oakley named her new non-profit company, Global Gardens. She had the name trademarked and is currently the CEO and President. Global Gardens and Eugene Field work side by side. The garden sits directly on our property. The kids grow their own vegetables, and Heather helps them sell their produce at the local farmer's market. 100 percent of all my third, fourth, and fifth graders have passed the Oklahoma state science test the last three years and I credit the work they are doing with Global Gardens. The students are gaining hands-on learning skills that will help them not only pass a test, but will help them with life skills. Global Gardens helps the children grow as people and productive members of society.

Working late for the third night in one week, I looked at the clock and it read 9:45 p.m. I packed my things away, hoping to get home to spend a little quality time with my husband and son before

I crashed for the night. I walked out into the night, heading for my car, when I heard laughing, talking, and giggling. I looked over and saw movement in the garden. I was immediately alarmed. I dumped my things in my car and stomped over to the garden to find three of my students.

"What in the world are you guys doing here at this hour?" I demanded.

More than a little taken aback that their principal was still at school, three children all looked at me in stunned silence and surprise until one of my third graders, Kimberly Hause, piped up. In a rush, Kimberly explained why she was there, "Ms. Hemm, it hasn't rained in three days and I was absent today because I had to take care of my baby brother because he was sick and my mama said I had to stay home because she was tired and I was worried about my garden because Ms. Oakley said my garden needed a drink of water every day and I didn't get to give my garden a drink today so I asked my friends if they wanted to come over here and help me give my garden a drink." Kimberly blew out a breath and ambled on, "and anyways, Ms. Oakley said we could come spend time with our gardens any time we wanted!"

I softened as I looked at them, all eyes wide as saucers, thinking they were in trouble.

"You students are so sweet to come give your gardens a drink, but it is way past your bedtimes. It is a school night tonight, and your brains need to sleep so you can be rested for tomorrow's activities. Of course, you can come see your garden any time, but right now you need sleep. Do your parents know where you are?"

"Mine are asleep," one answered.

"My parents aren't home," said another.

"Mine are working," explained the third child.

It was beyond me that three third graders were out unsupervised at 10 p.m. I sighed and said, "Thank you for giving your garden a drink. Now go home and sleep, and I will see you all in the morning."

"Okay, Ms. Hemm," they called as they ran back toward their apartments; Kimberly lingered behind as if she wanted to ask another question. "Is there something else you need, Kimberly?"

"Ms. Hemm, do you live here? I mean, do you live at the school, like sleep here?"

I couldn't help myself from laughing out loud, "I might as well, Kimberly. I am here a lot, but no, I don't sleep here."

"I thought it might be fun to sleep at school, and then I could be with my garden all the time. Well, see ya, Ms. Hemm!"

As I watched Kimberly run back to her apartment, I stood for a few quiet moments at the edge of our beautiful, viable community garden and thought what a blessing it was. Kimberly and her friends made me see what an impact Heather Oakley and Global Gardens were having on my students and their families. The garden is accessible twenty-four hours a day and seven days a week. The people of the community know they are always allowed to spend time with the garden any time they want.

Heather now employs seven educators. We have two of them at our building and five others throughout the city. After beginning at Eugene Field in 2005, Heather and Global Gardens began, branching out to different schools in the area. Today she is helping the whole community of Tulsa, because of a garden she started right beside Eugene Field Elementary. She has grown and flourished as the CEO and president of Global Gardens, a wonderful non-profit serving not only our community but the entire community of Tulsa.

In five years since the garden was first plowed, I am extremely proud to say, we had not a single incident of vandalism in the garden. Why? The people of this community would never vandalize something of which they were so proud.

As I walk by the garden several times a day, I often think to myself how I never asked for permission to have it. Personally, I don't think it is on anybody's radar that I bent the rules a little bit to help serve the people who live near our school. The Governor of Oklahoma, Mayor of Tulsa, and many members of the Tulsa philanthropic community have toured our garden. I haven't heard a word about my positive deviance when it came to establishing this gorgeous, functional, well-intentioned, garden that helps our community and gives them such pride and joy.

CHAPTER FIFTEEN

The Eugene Field Foundation

I arrived at school one early Thursday morning when the sun was just rising. It was cold outside. The previous night, I'd been unable to sleep, unable to shut off the thoughts of school and my very long "to-do" list. The list never seemed to dwindle; it grew longer and longer. After tossing and turning and realizing sleep would not come, I got up at 5 a.m. and headed over to my school.

Arriving just after 6 a.m., waiting outside the door was a mother of several of my students. Nancy Bowers, a mother of three, stood shivering by the locked door.

"Nancy," I said, "Are the children okay? Are you okay?"

"Ms. Hemm," she began, "the children are fine, but not for long. Our electricity has been out for weeks, and it's been so cold outside we have been trying to sleep in our car. Now we've run out of gas. I have no way to get to work, because I have no money to put gas in my car. No work means no money, and no money means no electricity in our apartment. I need help."

Sick to my stomach upon learning that this family had been sleeping in their car in freezing temperatures I asked them all to come in to school. I made the kids comfortable with a snack and some hot chocolate, and I pulled out my check book.

"Nancy, I'm giving you the money to get your heat turned back on," I said, "but, honey, I need you to keep working hard to provide for your family. Can you do that?"

"Yes, ma'am," she said gratefully. "Ms. Hemm, thank you, how can we ever pay you back?"

"As soon as it gets warm enough, you can help weed our front flower beds. Then we will call it even."

The first warm day in March, Nancy Bowers, on hands and knees, was pulling weeds out of the flower beds in front of our school. She was one person in a line of many who I helped with my own personal check book. My husband would often tease me, "Cindi, who did we tithe to this week?" Jeff knew I would answer with some version of, "We gave money to the Smith family for their water bill!" I often thought to myself, "I guess I will never be rich because I keep giving my money away! But, hey, you can't take it with you in the long run!"

For several years I continued to give away my own money for different emergencies including, but not limited to rent, gas money, hospital bills, electric bills, and food. We had two children of our own whom we were still providing for, one in college, and one still at home. I started re-evaluating how much money I was giving away. Therefore, the Eugene Field Foundation was born.

There were often times people off the street would come to me and say "Here is a hundred dollars to help some of your families." Members of First United Methodist Church, as well as many people in the Tulsa community, would hand over money, 50, 200, 1,000 even 5,000 dollars, or more to help our school in any way. Knowing we couldn't have money floating around the building, being that it is illegal and all, a foundation was formed. Margaret James, a Eugene Field teacher, volunteered her lawyer father, to draw up the legal papers and do all the work for the foundation pro bono. Margaret was a driving force behind the development of the foundation; she made certain that all activities were legal. An official non-profit, we filled out the paperwork, and made it official. I hired a director and we went from there.

I sat down with my new Eugene Field Foundation Director, Jeremy Martin, and we hashed out the particulars. He would be in charge of fundraising and would take care of all the funds in our foundation.

I still had to be smart about the money I was doling out. I am very cautious and wary about being taken advantage of. One of the reasons the Foundation is successful is because we know each and every family in this community extremely well. Through daily experience, we know who will take advantage of us and who will not. We always help children, but sometimes we can't help the adults in their lives who have made such poor choices.

Now when parents come to me and say, "I need money to pay my electric bill, my rent, my grocery bill." Our school foundation has the ability to help them. I do, however, always give them some type of chore to do around the school: weed the garden, clean the lunch room, or help pick up the gym toys.

Despite the resources of the foundation, I haven't become a rich woman. I found other ways to give my money away. I give several dollars to the homeless man who lives under the bridge every day on my way to school. I give to my church. I buy food, clothes, shoes, coats, and anything else for whoever may need them. Old habits die hard.

Even now when I get home from school and throw my bags on the kitchen table, my husband saunters in and winks at me, "Hey honey, who did we tithe to today?" I'm always able to come up with someone I handed cash to that day.

Countless people in Tulsa will hear about Eugene Field and wander in to see what the hype is all about. I give them a tour, and more often than not God moves their heart, to help us either monetarily or with gifts of their time and energies. The Eugene Field Foundation continues to help the people of this community because God has His mighty hand on us and we like it that way.

CHAPTER SIXTEEN

C-I-N-D-I -H-E-M-M Spells Advocate

When I first came to Eugene Field Elementary, there were three businesses who would occasionally give to the school. It wasn't enough. Our students needed more. I hit the ground running and started advocating on behalf of my school to any business or church in the area that would listen.

I started contacting the older Boy Scout troops, the Eagle Scouts. I told their leaders that we needed help. Soon here came these young men and their fathers asking, "What kind of projects do you have for us?"

In 2010 we have had twelve Eagle Scout projects completed at our school. Anything we needed they did, shape structures, building outdoor classrooms, painting, to name a few.

When I walked into the old building for the first time, I saw there were no stalls for little boys in the bathroom. I couldn't believe my eyes. As a mother of five children, three of them being boys, I was appalled.

"Where is the privacy for the boys?" I asked Tulsa Public Schools.

"Oh Cindi, don't worry! You are going to get a new building in a few years, and I'm sure they will build stalls for the boys in that building."

"What? Unacceptable! I'm going to fix this on my own!"

I was in disbelief, ranting and raving, having a fit! I couldn't get Tulsa Public Schools to get me some stalls for the boys so they could have a bowel movement in private.

I drove across town to a "rich" school. Wealthy oil barons lived in their Tulsa neighborhoods in the 1920's and many wealthy Tulsans live there still. Huge mansions and massive lots surround their school. Their school had central heat and air and stalls in the boys' bathrooms, something my school had neither of.

I set up a meeting with the PTA of the school in this prosperous neighborhood.

"Come to my school, Eugene Field, and see for yourselves the horrible shape the building is in. Our little boys' bathroom has no stalls. There is no privacy for them. They need a stall, and I need your help in getting one!"

These affluent parents came in droves to see our old building. Shocked at what they saw with their own eyes, they began calling Tulsa Public Schools and advocating for all our poor children as they would their very own. Soon after, Tulsa Public Schools purchased a stall for my little boys' bathroom. All the wives of the lawyers, oil and gas businessmen, and doctors who volunteered with their PTA adopted us.

I then turned my attention outside. All that sat in the middle of some dirt, sand, and gravel, walking out to what was called Eugene Field's "playground," if you could call it that, were three rusted barrels, and a set of monkey bars from the 1950's. That's it!

"This isn't proper playground equipment," I complained. I learned that the former principal was actually given money for new playground equipment, but she refused it and gave the money back to the district. She thought that the "poor" kids didn't need fancy equipment.

So angry, I was red-in-the-face mad, I wanted to shout, yell, and buy the equipment myself. My argument has always been that the children living in poverty need more money and better equipment, because they aren't getting the experiences that middle class and affluent children do.

Remembering the help the mothers of the school across town gave us, I got on the phone and asked for their help once more. They did a fundraiser for brand new playground equipment. The students of Eugene Field were thrilled.

Situated in our brand new building, I noticed another disturbing situation. Our school sits on a very busy, four-lane street, where 42,000 cars speed by every day. I watched as four-year olds and kindergartners shot across the busy street to get to school. Most parents, sleeping, working or unavailable, were not walking their kids to school. No one was using the 'near-by' pedestrian bridge because it was located half a mile down the road. We needed some assistance for students to keep them safe on their way to and from school each day.

I called the media, did an interview, and did my best to get flashing lights installed to slow down traffic, but no one would listen to me. During the interview I commented, on camera, that the City of Tulsa evidently cared only about the wealthy children at the rich school across town as they had two sets of flashing lights and three crossing guards. My bosses and the Tulsa Public Schools administration were not happy that I spoke so boldly on the issue. Called into the assistant superintendent's office, I spoke before anyone could scold me.

"Okay, ninety five percent of me is really good, but five percent of me needs to be reigned in. I get it!" I said, only half joking.

"Cindi, you cannot go on television and say that the city of Tulsa doesn't care about your kids."

After my small slap on the hand by Tulsa Public Schools, we were able to sit down and talk about the need for flashing lights at Eugene Field.

For the next four long years, I tried to get flashing lights installed on the busy street in front of Eugene Field to no avail. My complaints fell on deaf ears. The affluent school across town had two sets of flashing lights, three crossing guards, in addition to many parents who walked their children to school. "Hello! Tulsa, what about my students?"

I would not give up. I am an advocate. At every speaking engagement, I told the audience about how desperately we needed flashing lights to indicate our school zone and to slow the busy traffic on the street in front of Eugene Field.

"We need them before a child gets seriously injured or killed!"

I was invited to speak at an affluent private school named Holland Hall, located in a really nice part of Tulsa. I was asked to speak at their morning chapel, and I was to speak to a crowd of high school students.

I was getting pretty good at speaking in front of crowds and by this time I had been all over Tulsa advocating for my school.

I walked into Holland Hall early one morning ready to speak to a chapel full of teenagers. They walked in in their jackets and ties. Here sat the wealthiest people's children of Tulsa.

I began by saying, "Children of privilege, it is time to give back to your community just like your parents have been doing for years!" Four boys sitting in the front row rolled their eyes at me as I began to speak.

"I'm sorry, gentlemen, but you don't get to roll your eyes at me. If you don't want to hear what I have to say, then please feel free to exit the building."

They straightened right up and said, "Yes, ma'am."

All the students who started out not listening began to perk up as I spoke about Eugene Field.

"My students at Eugene Field Elementary aren't worried about the same types of problems you are. Prom, football games, the homecoming parade is nowhere near their thoughts and worries. Though these children live only fifteen minutes from here, less than ten miles away, they worry about where their next meal will come from or whether or not they will be warm at night while they try to sleep. Yesterday I had a kindergartner in my office who sat crying for over an hour because of cigarette burns all up and down her legs. The burns were from cigarettes that her mama's "johns" had put out on her. This is abuse like you have never seen in your lives."

I described another small child curled up in my office on a bean bag chair, her spine sticking so far out of her back simply because she didn't have enough food to eat. I told the story of my busy street and our lack of flashing lights and crossing guards.

"Children of privilege, hear me now. It. Is. Your. Turn. To. Give. Back. It is time to stand up and do something. You have such poverty in your own backyard. It is great to give to other causes overseas, but the children in my school are hungry, starving, abused, suffering things many of you have never imagined. It is your turn to give back to others! We need you!"

By the time I was finished, you could hear a pin drop.

After my speech at Holland Hall, I was packing up my things and shaking hands with a few people when a sweet little blonde girl came bouncing up to me.

"Ms. Hemm, I think I can help you get your flashing lights," she said.

"Good luck, honey, because I have been trying to get them for four years."

"Well, I'm on the Mayor's youth council, and my dad knows the Mayor really well," she explained.

That is all I needed to hear to perk me right up.

"Okay, sweetie, tell me everything!"

The blonde teenager was Annie Levoi, a strong-willed, dynamic personality who will one day change the world. I wouldn't be surprised if one day I will call her President Levoi.

Annie started attending meetings with the Mayor and asked for our flashing lights starting in January of 2006. She asked in January, February, March, and April. By April she raised her hand and said, "Mayor Taylor, I have been asking for these lights for four months now. I don't understand why we have a youth council if we can't get something done!"

Mayor Kathy Taylor looked at Annie, pointed her finger at her, and said, "Done!"

We had our flashing lights a week later. The lights slow down traffic, and now our students are safe crossing the street by themselves to get to school.

Annie is a phenomenal young lady and continues to have a relationship with Eugene Field Elementary. Currently attending America University in Washington D.C., she comes to visit us as often as she can. She mentored one of our students for years, helped to shape her life for the better, and keeps in touch with her to this day. She is a positive role model and I'm proud to know her. Annie Levoi did in four months what I couldn't get done in four years. Thanks, Annie! You rock!

Three adopters when I started have grown into over twenty-four businesses or churches who give Eugene Field Elementary everything from money to food to service. People are inherently good and want to help. At the very least and sometimes the very most, these businesses and organizations are hitting their knees for our school. Yes, our school, students, and staff are in their prayers.

I always say it is "dangerously joyful" to be among my friends or family because I will definitely and persistently ask you to be a part of my school as a mentor, to help serve at the community dinners, or to adopt our school. You will be invited to come help in any way you can possibly help at the best school in the whole wide world. All my best friends are there, and every single one of my family members has helped in some way. My sister is currently our mentor coordinator. Everyone contributes.

As I pray daily for my school and our families, I get a vision of a volcano erupting with the Holy Spirit throughout our building, throughout this community, through the city of Tulsa, through the state of Oklahoma, throughout the United States of America and through the world. I believe in the power of prayer and the goodness of people. Together, I know we can change the world, starting right here at Eugene Field Elementary.

CHAPTER SEVENTEEN

Presents on Christmas

Christmas is such a special time. When my own children were growing up, we had such rich traditions. Putting up the tree while listening to the Oakridge Boys Christmas CD, going to see the lights all over Tulsa, visiting with Santa at Woodland Hills Mall, and attending church on Christmas Eve to name a few. My kids would sit at the dining room table and write letters to Santa. It was music to mine and my husband's ears on Christmas morning to listen to the excited pitter-pat of feet down our stairs and the squeals of delight as they ripped open their presents. My own children grew up so fast, and now every Christmas my adult children, with grandchildren in tow, descend upon our house. We keep our rich traditions alive.

At Christmas time, I wanted something special for our Eugene Field babies as well. When I first came to Eugene Field Elementary, I found out some presents were donated at Christmas time, so some kids got presents, but some didn't. That didn't seem right to me. I made it my goal to get every child three gifts: a book, a toy, and an article of clothing.

I learned the hard way about giving to children who exist in poverty. If any tags remain on a new item some children's parents will see that their child has a valuable item that can be returned to the store in exchange for money. Then some of the adults use that money for something for themselves, leaving the child with nothing. However, if tags are removed and presents are given directly to the child, then it seems to work better for the children.

We worked hard to get over 1,000 presents donated for Christmas. The kids were ecstatic to receive their gifts at a special assembly the day before we dismissed classes for Winter Break.

Each year as I walk into the holiday assembly, their shinning, excited faces make my heart swell in my chest. We always have 100 percent attendance on this particular day.

"Good morning, boys and girls! What a great day we are going to have today!" A loud noise from the roof interrupts my greeting. THUMP, KERTHUMP, THUMP!

"Oh my goodness," I exclaim. "What could that possibly be on our rooftop?"

Delighted screams of "Santa and his reindeer" fill the auditorium! A volunteer dressed in full Santa gear bursts into our gym with bags and bags of presents. We witness the children's sheer delight as they jump up and down and begin clapping.

Thrilled, every student leaves with three gifts: a book, a toy, and an article of clothing. Every child is treated the same. Everything is equal.

Gearing up for our third annual Christmas assembly celebration, a grandmother of one of my first grade students, Michael Leroy, walked into my office and sat down.

"Ms. Hemm," she began, "I know you will give Michel three presents today and he is very excited. But I was wondering if you could give me his presents instead?"

"Why?" I questioned.

"As you know, Michael's mama has been real sick and his daddy is nowhere to be found. I've been raisin' that boy for the past two years and I always been able to get him at least one present on Christmas morning. But this year I ain't got nothing to give him, so I was wondering if I could have the presents you are going to give him today and put them under our small tree so he would have something to open on Christmas morning."

"That is a good idea, but then Michael will be the only one who wouldn't get presents today. He would probably feel really sad about that, don't you think?" I explained, "I have a better idea. How about Michael opens his three presents today with the other students, and I will find something to bring you that Michael can open on Christmas morning."

"Thank you Ms. Hemm," she sobbed, "I knew I could count on you."

I ran in every direction and found three more presents for my sweet first grader, Michael Leroy, who otherwise would have had nothing to open on Christmas morning. At 2 p.m. we knocked on Michael's grandmother's apartment door. Sure enough, I placed three presents, the only three presents they had under their small tree.

I hugged his grandmother.

"Merry Christmas!"

People all over the city of Tulsa make sure the students of Eugene Field have over 1,000 gifts to take home on Christmas. At times the only presents they have to open are the ones generous people have donated to our school. Why? Because Jesus is the "reason for the season" and He says to give and we do.

CHAPTER EIGHTEEN

The Mentor Tree

When I first came to Eugene Field there was a program called First Friends. Forty to fifty people from First United Methodist Church came in weekly to mentor children. This program was started by Don and Emily Renberg with the help of Connie Cole Jeske, all members of First United Methodist Church. I thought it was a great idea, but our students needed more mentors. I wanted the mentors we did recruit to commit to coming once a week without fail to meet with their chosen students.

We did a major push all over the city and grew fifty mentors into over two hundred and fifty people wanting and willing to be mentors at Eugene Field Elementary. I am praying that the day will come when every single one of our 430 students will have a mentor.

There is what is known as a discipline triangle in every school. Typically, five percent of kids are out of control, no matter what. Five percent of children are always in trouble. Fifteen percent have three or four referrals, while eighty percent of students are never in trouble. Statistically, every school has a discipline triangle.

Well, we had a discipline diamond back in 2003 when I began my journey as the principal at Eugene Field. We had twenty-five percent of the student population who were always in trouble and out of control. There were twenty-five percent who never got in trouble, and about fifty percent that had five to eight referrals.

We needed to move our student discipline picture from a diamond to a triangle, but how?

I started putting mentors with our toughest kids, thinking it would help these children who were constantly in trouble to have a positive role model in their lives.

Working hard one day, like always, I was called down to the cafeteria because two of my fifth grade girls were in a fist fight.

Running down the hall I threw open the doors to the lunch room to find Tara Wellborn and McKenna Rice, both throwing punches that would put Mike Tyson to shame. As I pulled them off each other, I was shocked to see McKenna in the midst of a fight. McKenna was a little girl who was never in trouble and who earned decent grades. Tara, on the other hand, had been in my office twice in the last week. Tara was a little girl we had paired with a wonderful mentor. Wanting to get to the bottom of this mess, I hauled them both into my office and talked with them separately.

"Tara, what in the world happened?" I questioned.

"Ms. Hemm, she started it. Came up to me pushin' and sayin' she knew I stole her bracelet! I ain't never seen no bracelet, I swear it!"

Tara finished relaying her side of the story to me, and I sent her to the nurse's office to get checked out. I pulled McKenna in to get her version.

"McKenna, I am very disappointed in you. You haven't been in trouble all year. What gives?"

"Ms. Hemm," she broke down in shameful tears, "Tara didn't steal my bracelet. I made it up."

"Why would you make such a thing up, McKenna, and start a fight?"

"It's not fair!" She sobbed, "Every week Tara gets to have Sonic cheese burgers with her mentor because she starts fights all the time.

I never get in trouble, but I never get Sonic cheese burgers. I thought maybe if I got in one fight, then I would get a mentor too!"

A light went off in my head. It took a fifth grader to help me see the error of my ways.

Immediately, I started pairing volunteer mentors with kids who were doing well. It is a privilege to have a mentor. Being completely honest with myself, I acknowledge that every student in our community needed a mentor. We paired the mentors with the students who behaved themselves, and all of a sudden I had the discipline triangle I was aiming for. This tactic made other kids work hard so they, too, could have a mentor.

Once a week, usually on Thursday or Friday, the mentors descend upon our building with lunch in tow. After lunch they play games with the students in the hallways. Everyone sees them. It is a fun, positive thing to have a mentor.

Every mentor gets a background check. Men are assigned to boys, and women are placed with girls. Each volunteer mentor serves as a positive adult role model who is employed, has a heart for children, and genuinely enjoys and cares about them. Every mentor must commit to spending at least thirty minutes a week with the student to whom he or she is assigned. Thirty minutes may not seem like a lot of time, but it can be. In only thirty minutes a week, volunteer mentors are changing students' lives at Eugene Field for the better. Sometimes that is all it takes.

CHAPTER NINETEEN

Pieces of the Puzzle

Many miracle workers have accomplished great things at Eugene Field. Sometimes we are assisted by individuals who are called into service at Eugene Field Elementary who stay but only a little while. Sometimes people are called to do their life's work at our school, where they perform miracles every day. Both are essential in making Eugene Field a well-rounded school.

My first year working at Eugene Field, I hired a famous local artist named Matt Moffit. Matt was our art teacher for three years. He is a fabulous artist who also happened to teach. Currently, we have a great teacher who happens to be a wonderful artist. There is a difference. I knew Matt wouldn't be with us for long because his heart was to paint. He served as a wonderful teacher. He worked with the children, directing them as they created the most beautiful pieces of artwork I have ever seen. Matt put his mark on our school because all around us are wonderful reminders of the work he used to do with our children.

Matt came to me one day and said he would like to help the children build an Art Garden behind the school. He had found a plot of land behind the school and fenced it off. For months the children worked, under Matt's direction, and they built the Art Garden that currently resides behind our school.

The beautiful Art Garden has cut-outs of Mona Lisa, magnificent painted structures, art projects of different sizes, shapes and color. It is another aspect of Eugene Field Elementary in which the kids have taken great pride and ownership. Never once have I ever seen a piece of trash or graffiti in the Art Garden. The children and their parents are proud of their accomplishments, and the Art Garden is an outside reminder of how the whole community takes care of this school.

The Art Garden represents the peacefulness and calm that enriches the entire school every day. Thanks, Matt!

Before my tenure as administrator of Eugene Field, the school had a project funded through First United Methodist Church called the Big Bucks Store. In a trailer beside the school, the Big Bucks Store is filled with candy, toys, soap, conditioner, personal hygiene products, trinkets, and basic needs items.

Students earn "Big Bucks" by coming to school every day, by being on time, dressing in their uniforms, and being kind and respectful. Every other week, students may spend their 'big bucks' on items in the store.

As our school grew and grew, so did our Big Bucks Store. First United Methodist Church donates about $5,000 dollars a year for items for the store. Bargain shopping volunteers search the Tulsa area for items offered at low prices and bring them back to the Big Bucks Store. Children buy their birthday and Christmas presents for their friends and family with their 'big bucks.' Volunteers help them wrap their purchased items.

The Big Bucks Store provides a wonderful incentive for good behavior and also a invaluable life lesson, "Work hard, get rewarded and paid, provide for your family." Those are valuable lessons to teach elementary school children living in generational poverty.

In my previous middle class school we would hold food drives to give food to families in great need. All of a sudden, I found myself in the midst of a community of people who were very much in need. We began doing food drives with our school business partners and other schools in the area to stock a food pantry for the Eugene Field community.

Right next to the Big Bucks Store is our Food Pantry, stocked with non-perishable food items such as canned goods, pasta, and canned meats.

At the end of the month, when the need is the greatest, parents come in droves to get food from the pantry that will last them until they get their next round of food stamps.

When we first started the Food Pantry, one of our many volunteers gave a mom of one student a bag of pinto beans in her sack of food. Cooking is a lost art among many of the parents of Eugene Field, so the mom brought the bag of pinto beans back to us and said, "These beans have gone bad! We can't eat this!" I brought this parent back in the food pantry, wrote down a recipe, gave her a big pot, and taught her how to cook the beans.

From that day on, we remember to always give the parents a recipe and teach them how to cook food for their families. We are not only helping them out, but we are helping them up.

CHAPTER TWENTY

A Community Grocery Store

Being the white middle class suburban-living woman that I am, I would often take for granted the easy access made available to me by way of groceries for my family. I jump in the car that I own, drive to one of the nearest grocery stores, load up on food items, drive back home and unload groceries from my car to my refrigerator. After working at Eugene Field for several years, however, I no longer take for granted my middle class existence.

Getting into my car late one evening, I watched the city bus pull up to one of the apartment complexes next to the school. I watched as a grandmother, guardian of four small children because mom was in jail, trying to carry grocery bags, hold the hand of her youngest child, while trying to get off the bus. Juggling milk containers and macaroni and cheese boxes, she stumbled down the steps of the bus. I immediately ran over to help her.

"Hi, Ms. Hemm," she said, "Thank you for helping."

"Ms. Combs," I questioned, "Is this how you get groceries for your family?"

"Ms. Hemm, there ain't no stores 'round here to walk to, and I ain't got no car. I have to take this city bus here every other Tuesday with three different bus exchanges just to get here and back from the Wal-mart'cross town. I can't get very much 'cause I gotta take all my kids with me, and carryin' four babies and Wal-mart bags just don't work real well."

"What about the convenience store around the corner?" I asked.

"No way, Ms. Hemm, have you ever been in there? It stinks to high heaven, real dirty, real expensive, and the milk spoils real fast."

As we walked to her apartment carrying her grocery bags, I was shocked to learn she once paid a "friend" fifteen dollars to drive her to a grocery store ten miles across town. Coming back out of the store with her family's groceries, her "friend" had left her there with no ride home. She picked out the groceries she knew were necessities and walked the ten miles home. Ever since, she had been taking the city bus every other week to buy food for her family.

Leaving her apartment that night, I stopped at the disreputable convenience store around the corner. Walking in the door, I was immediately taken aback by the smell of rotten eggs and urine. My shoes stuck to the dirty floor as I walked to the back of the store. The prices were ridiculously high. That's great, I thought to myself, let's gouge the poor people. Half a gallon of milk was five dollars. I picked up a carton of milk, saw it was two weeks past the expiration date, and stormed up to the counter. Standing in line to have a word with the manager I noticed there were condoms and dirty magazines for sale, displayed at eye level, for a ten year old to see.

"Excuse me, did you know this milk is old and the price isn't right? Are you the manager?"

The man didn't speak a word of English as I tried and failed to explain to him that his store was price gouging.

I left feeling frustrated and pissed off!

Driving home that night, I knew in my mind we needed a grocery store. I started advocating at every speaking engagement to any business or church who would listen.

"We need a grocery store!" I would plead. "The only way to buy food is to get on a city bus with several transfers in order to get to a store across town." Relaying the experience I had with Ms. Combs was just one example of families trying to buy food. "The only places to buy food are the McDonalds or Sonic down the street from my students' apartments. There is nowhere else to go. We have entire generations who have only eaten fast food. Our four-year old students walk into my building having eaten nothing but French fries and hamburgers. Never once have they eaten a home-cooked meal with fresh vegetables or fruit. Sometimes there is no food at all and they just go without. We need a grocery store!"

One day the Lord intervened.

I was sitting at my desk, racking my brain about the little girl currently asleep on the bean bag chair on my office floor. I was out of my mind with worry about her. She was one of the worst cases of abuse I had ever seen at Eugene Field. She came to school crying, with cigarette burns all up and down her legs, cigarette burns that her mother's "johns" had put out directly on her. I looked at her while she slept, rail thin, bones protruding from her body, hungry and abused; her scars ran so much deeper than what her burns were showing. I sat with my head in my hands until I heard a knock at my door.

"Hi, Ms. Hemm, I'm Clark Millspaugh. My wife and I used to mentor here some time ago, and I would like to talk to you about starting up again."

"Hi, Clark, yes, I remember hearing about you. You are a member of First United Methodist Church. We would love for you and your wife to begin mentoring again."

Clark looked over and saw the little girl on the bean bag chair for the first time. He asked, "What has happened to her?"

"She is homeless, very abused and hungry. We are trying to teach her to read and write, but in the meantime all she is trying to do is survive."

As I explained to him the abuse she had suffered, he reached down and patted her on the back. Clark felt her spine protruding from her back. He put his hand over his mouth, gasped, and began to cry.

"Cindi, this moves my heart in way you will never know. This day will be with me always. What can I do to help make things a little better for these children?"

"Clark, these people need a grocery store." I explained, "Somewhere within walking distance which offers affordable groceries."

Clark nodded his head, picked up his things, got into his car and drove around our school. Behind our property sat two yellow, steel buildings. It had been a place where race cars were built many years ago, but now these buildings just sat off to the side of Eugene Field Elementary with a foreboding barbed wire fence around them. Clark Millspaugh saw something in those buildings that day, he got immediately on the phone with the man who owned the buildings. Clark made that man an offer he couldn't refuse. Clark and a group of investors bought the buildings for $250,000.

With another $250,000 dollars, Clark and his investors renovated the buildings. Clark oversaw every aspect of creating the West Side Harvest Market, a non-profit grocery store. The store accepts food stamps and sits directly on the Eugene Field property. It is open five days a week from 10 a.m. to 6 p.m., and is operated by volunteers. The West Side Harvest Market carries milk, bread, vegetables, and other good wholesome food to make good wholesome meals at affordable prices. It is a Christian place, run by people with a heart for the Lord.

Clark Millspaugh belongs to a group called the "Half Time Club." Their philosophy is that you make money the first half of your life, and you make a difference the second half. He puts his money where his mouth is. A man of great faith, Clark is making such a big difference in the lives of the people in this community. Through Clark's relationships and connections throughout the Tulsa area, he has brought and continues to bring many people into service at Eugene Field. I call this the Lord's tapestry. In other words, all of us have a thread in this life, and no one knows what this beautiful, completed picture will look like. You just have to pick up your thread and continue to weave your destiny.

Next door to the store is a teaching kitchen where teachers from Eugene Field teach their students how to cook. With full access to the kitchen, the teachers teach the children how to measure ingredients, bake, and how to eat quality wholesome food. The children are thrilled when they make zucchini bread or blueberry muffins from scratch.

Global Gardens also has a classroom in the building. Global Gardens works directly with the West Side Harvest Market, where the students can sell their home-grown vegetables in the store.

The other building has four ministries working directly from it. It has a 24-hour prayer room dedicated by none other than the man who started the national 24-hour prayer movement, Pete Gregg. The prayer room is a place of peace and quiet. The ambience of the prayer room is serene with lowly lit lights, couches, soft music playing, Bibles to read, and many different places to meditate. Next door to the prayer room, there is a place for seven missionaries to live and serve the families in the Eugene Field community.

The West Side Harvest Market, teaching kitchen, Global Gardens classroom, 24-hour prayer room, and residences for missionaries and work space happened because a hungry, homeless, abused little girl was curled up on my floor sleeping without anyone to love her but me and the warriors God has sent into service at my school.

CHAPTER TWENTY-ONE

More Programs Get Results

A pervasive movement across the nation, Positive Behavior Support is a growing educational program which encompasses many of the aspects that make Eugene Field Elementary a successful school. We put together a PBS team which includes key members of the Eugene Field staff. In addition to incentives for the children, PBS emphasizes the use of common language and terminology coupled with common procedures. PBS has improved student behavior school-wide.

At Eugene Field, our PBS team is made up of a group of strong individuals with children's best interests in mind. Monthly team meetings are designed to put in place new procedures, evaluate current procedures, and to keep our kids on the right track. Because our students and their environments are ever-changing, we must also be ready to make continuous changes to help children get the best education we can give them. That means being open to change. Constantly striving and learning to do things better for our school, these open-minded teachers are in learning mode most of the time.

Our PBS school mantra is "STAR," an acronym that stands for "Students Thinking and Acting Responsibly." STAR helps the children and teachers stay positive. We use STAR tickets for children who attend school every day, and tickets are also given for acts of students caught thinking and acting responsibly. We have daily drawings, and the student winners get the privilege of going into the Big Bucks Store to pick out any item of their choice.

Our PBS team reviews and analyzes the student disciplinary records every month. Our school also participates in a website called "The Educator's Handbook" that tracks all of our disciplinary infractions. The data related to student disciplinary problems is analyzed by day, time, month, and year. We have been using it for three years.

In one of our monthly PBS meetings, we were reviewing the discipline data and noticed a spike in discipline around our state-mandated testing time. The PBS team brainstormed and came up with a plan to alleviate stress and reduce discipline problems during that time of year. We instituted a "theme week." While the older children were testing, the younger students were outside doing scavenger hunts, outdoor games, and activities. In the afternoon after the testing was over, the older children got to take a turn playing outside and doing a scavenger hunt. These special activities gave the students something to look forward to, and we saw vast improvements in our discipline problems. Positive Behavior Support has been an important tool in our school's improvement. Eugene Field is an official PBS school, and we are proud to be one!

Another educational initiative we adopted was the process to become an "A+ school." A national program that operates on the state level, A+ provides professional development to assist educators in integrating the arts into every classroom. Most educators realize that children learn so much through music, drama, poetry, and other art-related strategies. All the A+ schools in Oklahoma share resources and successes about the integration of the arts in the day-to-day curriculum in the classroom.

We enjoy a variety of artistic performances throughout the year. Thanks to A+, we also do "informances," where we inform our parents and community about what we are learning. Students show their parents and family members the latest in technology, like how to use a smart board. A+ has assisted us in fine-tuning our teaching practices.

We are fortunate enough to live in Oklahoma where our Governor, Brad Henry, and his wife Kim, a former educator, put great emphasis on education. I received a phone call in February of 2006.

"Cindi, this is Sally from the Oklahoma Department of Education. I wanted to be the first to congratulate you on your test scores doubling from last year. Your school will be receiving the Oklahoma State Academic Achievement Award! Each one of your certified staff gets a check for $2,000 dollars. Great work!"

Ecstatic, somewhere between happy tears and jumping up and down with joy, I sat down in my chair and thanked the Lord for this wonderful news. There was a knock at my office door.

"Come in," I said, as Abby Waters, one of the most phenomenal kindergarten teachers I have ever seen in action came walking into my door.

"Abby, you will not believe the phone call I just received. We are the recipients of the Oklahoma State Academic Achievement Award. Every certified teacher at Eugene Field will receive $2,000 dollars for doubling our test scores from last year!"

Abby screamed in delight, but then paused and looked at me in question.

"What about the support staff?" she asked. "They were as vital as we were in changing this school for the better. They are one of the reasons we are all successful. That is not fair!"

In true Abby form, always thinking about someone else, she got my wheels turning.

"That is true," I said, "We will figure something out."

The next day I assembled my teachers together and told them the news. Beyond humbled and grateful, they hugged each other. Some broke down in happy tears.

"Our support personnel, who have been as vital as you in our success, will receive no money for their part in this wonderful award. Therefore, I want to put a challenge out to each of you to tithe, to a pool for a monetary award to be shared by our support staff."

We passed around a large bowl for donations from our certified teachers. I was overwhelmed with joy when we were able to give each support person employed at our school $200 dollars each. This is just one example of the extraordinary people who work at our school. There are no better people and no better place to be than Eugene Field Elementary.

CHAPTER TWENTY-TWO

The Eugene Field Baby School

The Eugene Field community was becoming more cohesive. With an emphasis on our community school and the positive practices we put into place with our students, our school was becoming a coveted place to be. Still, we didn't get opportunity to work with our children until they were four years old.

I thought often about how we might get to the children earlier. The babies in this community grow up in generational poverty. They get fed sometimes. The television is always on. Their caregivers take care of the babies sometimes, but sometimes they are not cared for at all. We know that the time from birth to three years old is the most crucial time for children, the time where they form attachments and relationships, and learn to trust or mistrust their environment. I knew that this was a vital time period for babies, which sets them up for a lifetime of success or a lifetime of failure. I often wished that we could have a nursery or daycare on site where the babies of this community could attend for free, a place where babies could be cared for and where we could begin instilling the morals, values, and love we instill in our older children.

I started praying for God to send us help. Enter Steven Dow, the head of a community action project.

Steven came to me one day and said he wanted to build a Head Start program on our property, right behind our school.

"Steven," I said, "you are an answer to prayer. We so desperately need a Eugene Field Baby School."

Plans were made to begin construction on the Head Start program that I affectionately named "The Eugene Field Baby School" and the term stuck. The community was also ecstatic about the program, which would be an income-based program, free of charge to families.

In the fall of 2008, the project was complete. From infants to age three, 170 children were enrolled in the Eugene Field Baby School.

From the beginning plans through the construction of the building, we knew it was vitally important for the 'baby school' and the elementary school to present a united front to our community. If the 'baby school' was seen as an extension of Eugene Field Elementary, the community was more likely to have a positive outlook on this new endeavor. The leadership at the Eugene Field Early Childhood Center, i.e. "The Eugene Field Baby School," is wonderful. Director Paulette Kothe and I have quarterly meetings to discuss our progress and how we can assist each other. A year after the baby school opened Paulette called me.

"Cindi, we need to talk," she said. "Now don't shoot the messenger, but my bosses several levels above me have asked me to tell you to stop calling our school the "Eugene Field Baby School," that name is not accurate."

I doubled over with laughter. I laughed so hard my side ached.

"Paulette," I said still chuckling, "I don't do what my own bosses tell me to do, let alone what your bosses tell me to do!"

I thought it was hilarious. I had been calling the Head Start program the 'baby school' for the past five years, and so had everyone else in anticipation of the building finally opening.

That very next day, I purchased a shirt for every student at the baby school and emblazed on the front it said, "Eugene Field Baby School." We wear them proudly.

It is an ideal marriage between Eugene Field Elementary and the Head Start program built directly behind us. They enroll the babies when they are six weeks old, and the children continue to stay there until age three. Their three-year olds then transition out of the baby school into the elementary school. The Head Start is an excellent and successful program. The children are well-fed and cared for. They have books read to them, instrumental music playing, and a consistent schedule they can count on.

When the babies turn three, they start visiting the "big" school. Eugene Field fourth graders help the three-year olds get their lunches and play with them in the gym. When the babies turn four, they are more than comfortable in our building, and ready to start Pre-Kindergarten at the elementary school.

With consistent care and proper nutrition in a stimulating, age-appropriate environment, these babies are on the road to success at a very early age. When the children arrive at Eugene Field Elementary, they are receptive to what we are ready to teach them. The baby school helped stabilized our community.

CHAPTER TWENTY-THREE

Eugene Field's Rock Star Teachers: Our Test Scores Soar to the Top

I may be the administrator of Eugene Field Elementary, but I must give credit where credit is due. The teachers at our school are amazing. They epitomize the term "Rock Star Teachers!" Truly, 95 percent of my teachers are exceptional. In the past we have had a few weak teachers, but they have come and gone. At the beginning of each school year, I stand up in our first meeting and address the teachers.

"This is a hard place to teach. I want you to work beyond the hours required by your contract, before school, after school, and on the weekends. In doing that, we will support you. This is a family. This is a calling. If you need to take off, we will support you. If you are able to give all you've got for our students, the rewards are ten-fold. This is holy work. This is Eugene Field Elementary."

I have a leadership team in place that takes ownership of our school. I'm not a boss who says it's "my way or the highway." I listen to our staff and our leadership team. They run the school, and they are valued. If I make a suggestion or present an idea that everyone doesn't support, I'm okay with that; we go with a different plan, a better idea, or another suggestion. There isn't one person out there who knows all the answers. Seven heads are better than one, and I have tremendous faith in the dedicated people who lead our school.

In the middle of my first year at Eugene Field, one of our "rock star" teachers, who happened to be six months pregnant, came to me with concern in her eyes. "Ms. Hemm, we need to talk."

As she sat in front of me, she began to cry and explained that day care was too expensive. She wanted to be close to her baby, so she had decided she would not be returning to school after her maternity leave. I told her how much we would miss her, but that I understood her decision and to call me when she was ready to teach again. We hugged, and she went on her way.

Driving home that night, I felt great sadness about the loss of such a wonderful teacher. Why would an industry made up of 90 percent women not have nurseries in every school in America? It should be a requirement. We have high school girls having babies, and we support them with a special school where they can continue attending classes with on-site daycare. Why wouldn't we do that for our teachers, women who keep the education profession running? With school daycare, we wouldn't lose so many teachers who opted to stay home because of expensive day care and their desires to breastfeed and be close to their babies. The idea had taken root, and I decided right then and there to have a nursery installed at Eugene Field.

Our nursery works out perfectly. The teachers hire the nursery workers and pay them directly. We have a designated nursery in a classroom within our building with cribs, toys, changing stations, rocking chairs, and I get to keep my "new mama" teachers. They use their breaks to nurse their babies, and then return to teaching their classes. We celebrate their children growing up. We give them awards for bravery, first teeth, and first steps in our assemblies. The nursery workers put the babies in strollers and walk them around the school. They are valued members of our school. It is part of our family community culture.

To walk into Eugene Field at any time of day on any day of the week, you will see the most phenomenal teachers in the world in action. One can observe real life, hands-on teaching, active learning, interesting lessons and happy children in every single classroom, every single day. And it is not just the teachers who amaze me, but the whole staff at our school. Our office personnel are the kindest, most wonderful staff in Oklahoma. They work very hard and are always ready to help children, ready to help parents; they encompass the kind of qualities that are essential in making us successful. As I walk through the building each and every day I am humbled at the progress we have made. To every person on our faculty and staff, I thank you!

In June, 2008, our state achievement test scores arrived. We scored 1357 out of a possible 1500 points. We scored higher than most area schools, suburban schools, and affluent schools in Tulsa. In this way, we demonstrated that Eugene Field is a school that can stand up to any school in the nation. The teachers who work at Eugene Field Elementary could be picked up and put anywhere in any inner urban, high poverty school and be successful. The skills and strength possessed by each of my teachers are exceptional. Our teaching staff is so strong now that if a weak teacher were to join our staff, they will run an ineffective teacher out. Each teacher must be able to step up and do what it takes to get the job done successfully.

I call it a perfect storm. Putting together all of these practices have created an exceptional school. If this can be accomplished in our school, it can be done anywhere. We had naysayers, those people who didn't believe in the miracle that is Eugene Field Elementary. We showed them all. We were in the top ten percent of schools in the state because of our test scores. We had soared to the top.

CHAPTER TWENTY-FOUR

The End/The Real Beginning -
To God Be The Glory

The positive accomplishments, the resources, the family relationships, and our academic success continue to happen because this is God's school. God continues to work miracles and open doors in this community. Remember Marcus Lewis, my fifth grade former "deputy?" Next year, I will see Marcus and many of my former students from that tumultuous first year graduate from high school.

I often wander through the building with a smile on my face and a feeling of nostalgia, thinking back on my first few years at Eugene Field Elementary and how far we've come. Walking through our beautiful, state-of-the-art building, I can look out the window and see children working and learning in the community garden. I see parents filling up grocery bags at the West Side Harvest Market. I see "Rock Star Teachers" in action, with captivated students working on Target Teach lesson plans. I wave and say hello to mentors lining our halls, waiting for their chosen students to join them for lunch. I give a "thumbs-up" to a second grade class walking down the right side of the hall, each one with a bubble in their mouths, decked out in their school uniforms.

"Ms. Hemm, are you coming to our soccer game on Saturday?"

"Ms. Hemm, are you coming to my piano recital?"

"Ms. Hemm, I am so excited to perform my dance routine on Friday!"

All these activities have been made possible through this school and the warriors God has sent into service at Eugene Field.

I breeze into school on a Thursday morning. I throw my bags on the floor next to my desk and check a few emails. It is a good day. There is an excitement in the air because today is our annual spelling bee.

I walk into the assembly to see the shining faces of over 400 Eugene Field students.

"Good morning, boys and girls!" I exclaim. "Today is such a special day. Today is our spelling bee! May I have our spellers on stage, please!"

Applause erupts from the student body as the class spelling winners line the stage. Filled with pride, the class spelling bee champions take their seats. They look up and wave at their parents, who are lining the gym.

As the spelling bee begins, you can hear a pin drop. All the students are on the edge of their seats as they wait in anxious anticipation to find out who our spelling bee champion will be this year.

Only two spellers are left, Micah Hall and Destiny Jones. The word given is "exuberant" as Destiny walks to the microphone. Destiny looks at her mom, who yells out "E!" then sits down with a thud, very obviously embarrassed. I looked at the teacher in charge and said, "New word."

I walked over to Ms. Jones and she blurted out, "Ms. Hemm, I'm sorry. I just got so excited! It won't happen again." I chuckled and said jokingly, "I know, because I don't want to have to kick you out. It is too exciting!" I walked back up to the stage just in time for Destiny to be named the official winner.

The audience claps and yells cheers of respect and admiration as Destiny and her peers head back to class. I go back to my office and think about my first spelling bee at Eugene Field Elementary. Seven years ago, I would never have imagined how wonderful this school would eventually become.

As I walk the halls, I remember the fateful day my warriors and I wrote Scripture all over the foundation of this building, praying for protection, praying for light, praying for wisdom, strength and kindness. Don't get me wrong, we are still in the midst of one of the poorest areas in Tulsa. Yes, every day is tough, but we persevere. We believe in the miracle on Southwest Boulevard, the miracle that is our school and we rejoice in the miracle that is our lives, the miracle that is Eugene Field Elementary.

To God be the Glory.

Amen.

Cindi Hemm making rounds at Eugene Field Elementary

Historical column brought over to carefully
preserve the old building's memory

The new and improved state of the art Eugene Field Elementary

*Eugene Field students stand proudly
in front of their brand new school*

Hard at work in the Global Gardens

A Eugene Field fifth grade class preparing for their next lesson

A Eugene Field student picks out potatoes
at the Westside Harvest Market

Clark Millspaugh mentors students at Eugene Field Elementary

Ms. Samuelson's class poses for a class picture

Eugene Field students wear their new uniforms proudly

ABOUT THE AUTHOR

Ms. Cindi Hemm has been an educator in Tulsa Public Schools since 1982. She started her career with Tulsa as a speech pathologist and teacher. She has been a school administrator for the past 15 years.

In her current position as principal of Eugene Field Elementary, Ms. Hemm has overseen a dramatic change at a high-minority, high-poverty school that serves the children from several public housing projects in Tulsa. Through her leadership, Eugene Field has gone from having the lowest academic scores in the district to among the highest in the district and the state. Eugene Field was recognized as the most improved school in the Tulsa district. The school was subsequently recognized as one of the most improved in the state of Oklahoma.

Ms. Hemm's contributions go well beyond the academic program at the school. She has spearheaded efforts to address health and nutrition needs for her students and their families. She is a bold champion for her school and students, and has personally raised untold funds for needed school projects.

Ms. Hemm is an accomplished speaker, having presented at the National Title I Conference, National Staff Development Conference, the National Community Schools annual conference & Evans Newton Winter Symposium.

Ms. Hemm won District Administrator of the Year for Tulsa Public Schools in 2008 and 2010. Ms. Hemm was also the recipient of the 2011 Oklahoma Foundation for Excellence award.

She is a graduate of Nathan Hale High School and The University of Arkansas. She and her husband, Jeff, reside in Tulsa, Oklahoma.